T0248070

break
blow
burn
&
make

E. LILY YU

break
blow
burn
&
make

A WRITER'S THOUGHTS ON CREATION

New York   Nashville

Worthy

Hachette Book Group

1290 Avenue of the Americas, New York, NY 10104

worthypublishing.com

twitter.com/worthypub

First Edition: June 2024

Some of the chapters in this book adapt ideas or reuse material from "Against Authentic," which first appeared at *Locus* (2021), and the following essays that originally appeared on the author's Substack: "What is Missing, What is Gone," "On Privacy and Solitude," "The Courage of Making," "The Love of Words, the Love of Language," "On the Cost of All Things," and "On Precision."

Worthy is a division of Hachette Book Group, Inc. The Worthy name and logo are registered trademarks of Hachette Book Group, Inc.

The publisher is not responsible for websites (or their content) that are not owned by the publisher.

Worthy books may be purchased in bulk for business, educational, or promotional use. For information, please contact your local bookseller or the Hachette Book Group Special Markets Department at special.markets@hbgusa.com.

Copyright page continues on page 223.

Interior illustrations by E. Lily Yu

Print book interior design by Amy Quinn

Library of Congress Cataloging-in-Publication Data

Names: Yu, E. Lily, author.

Title: Break, blow, burn, and make : a writer's thoughts on creation / E. Lily Yu.

Description: First edition. | New York, NY : Worthy, 2024.

Identifiers: LCCN 2023046054 | ISBN 9781546005490 (hardcover) | ISBN 9781546005513 (ebook)

Subjects: LCSH: Creation (Literary, artistic, etc.)—Religious aspects. | Fiction—Authorship. | Christian life.

Classification: LCC PN3355 .Y84 2024 | DDC 808.3—dc23/eng/20231218

LC record available at https://lccn.loc.gov/2023046054

ISBNs: 9781546005490 (hardcover), 9781546005513 (ebook)

Printed in the United States of America

LSC-C

Printing 1, 2024

For my father,
who was wrong about

almost

everything

It burnt, it burns — my whole life burnt with it,
And light, not sunlight and not torchlight, flashed
My steps out through the slow and difficult road.

Elizabeth Barrett Browning, *Aurora Leigh*

break
blow
burn
&
make

I

Chapter One

AN ABSENCE SHAPED
LIKE FLAME

UNLIKE THE DECISION TO BEGIN LIVING, WHICH IS made for us, and which we embark upon in total ignorance and terror, the decision to keep bees, to write, or to follow Christ is usually made with a vague and incomplete idea of what will be required: a hive, a few notebooks and pens, or a hymnal and a church. Then three pounds of golden furred bodies arrive purring in their box, and it quickly becomes clear that in addition to the basic skills of building and inspecting a hive, a beekeeper ought to know woodworking, as well as how to light and stoke a fire in a smoker. The smoker, essentially a lidded tin can, allows the beekeeper to suggest that there is a wildfire about, and therefore that the bees have more important concerns than the person breaking into their home at that moment. A very bad time to discover one's own lack of fire-making skills is when the smoker, which moments ago had been puffing smoke, ceases to smoke entirely, leaving one standing in a cloud of irritable bees.

The tree overshadowing my home drops a sufficient number of dry twigs for my smoker, but they don't catch fire when touched to a lighter, even if one is wearing a scruff of oakmoss. Because I tend to have a church program or two lying around in my car, I tear those in half, crumple a piece, light it, and work the bellows until the slim orange line eating through the paper expands into flame. The twigs have to be laid over that, or they won't catch, and not all at once, or the flame goes out.

Only when the fire is sufficiently fed, a crown of flames leaping out of the smoker, do I cover it with the bracken fronds and zigzag stems of salal that I've trimmed from around the hive, producing a cool white smoke. Too much greenery on too weak a flame, and the smoker ceases to smoke at inopportune times.

A certain degree of order, both human and natural, goes into my smoker: prayers and birthday wishes printed on twenty-pound paper, lignin and cellulose arranged into pith, cambium, xylem, and phloem, and the tracery of veins on leaves. Through pyrolysis and combustion, producing light and heat along with the smoke, that complexity is broken down into smaller, simpler particles. After the fire goes out, what remains is ashes, soot, and charred fragments. Order becomes disorder; entropy increases locally; the universe advances toward chaos.

The kind of writing I think of as incandescent, and discuss in this book, resembles this process in reverse. The writer begins with light, which is sometimes a steady white flame, sometimes no more than an ember that must be blown to brightness, and the dust and ashes left by living one's life. Within and through the writer, this dust and that light combine to create the drafts of a book, one after another, each exhibiting an increasing internal order, like the instars of a dragonfly. If the process is carried to its final and most perfect point, a whole world emerges, richly complicated, well-ordered, and entire. The book blazes forth for as long as it has a chance of finding a reader. By reading it, we risk being set alight ourselves. But this fire does not disorder and destroy. Instead, if we let it, if we come close enough to catch fire, it burns through our preconceptions and our whole way of living, and increases the complexity, order, and richness of our lives.

This is the only sort of writing that interests me these days. It has never been common, though it shines out, here and there, from the heaps of books written for their times and left in those times.

What concerns me is that, as far as I can tell, that kind of writing has nearly vanished. For a decade, I put my head down to research, compose, revise, and eventually publish a difficult novel, in the crevices of time between full-time jobs, academic programs, other writing, and the demands of life, in the hope that I could add an affirming flame to the light thrown off by the writers I admired, whose words had lit my way. When I surfaced, after all of that, the world had changed. A light had gone out of the new books I was reading. They were sometimes entertaining, witty, competent, and comforting, and sometimes they were not, but they struck me as missing that vital flame.

In *The Captive Mind*, the poet Czesław Miłosz describes a reader pinned down by gunfire in the street, who observes cobblestones knocked upright by bullets hitting their edges. In that moment, he says, a great deal of celebrated poetry is revealed to that person as worthless. Only that poetry which is as real as the sight of those cobblestones will be judged worthwhile. Readers who have lived through such experiences of naked reality, Miłosz writes, are impatient with whatever is not firmly rooted in the real.[1] "They are hungry—but they want bread, not hors d'oeuvres."[2]

I also am hungry for the bread that Miłosz means, and too often fail to find it, unless I am looking to past decades. Christ called Himself the bread of life because He gives his followers nourishment, vitality, and the strength to do the work they are given for the day. I have found a comparable sustenance in the subset of books I have in mind, as well as much of Miłosz' poetry, and I believe that the resemblance is because they come from the same source. Most writers today have misplaced or mistaken that source, that sacred flame, in part because we rarely speak about it. The circumstances of life in the twenty-first century are, moreover, decidedly inhospitable to writing in this way. But hunger drives people to extraordinary lengths. Because of my hunger, I have written this book.

I observed other changes as well. Many books seemed riddled with anxiety, or else anger, that did not arise within the text but warped it from without. The shape of a sentence seemed to have melted like wax. Words were being slopped around, abused and misused, with the

1. "The real," or "reality," is not a matter of genre, and not related to realism. Miłosz himself was condemning social realism. Some fantasies have this quality, while much realistic fiction does not.
2. Czesław Miłosz, *The Captive Mind*, trans. Jane Zielonko (New York: Vintage, 1981), 41.

delicacy of paint applied by mortar trowel. And underneath all these signs was that gnawing absence.

One night in Chicago, I sat down to dinner with an editor, a critic, and a teacher, all of whom had felt that same ache and vacancy, and I named the loss aloud: love.

By love I mean what Erich Fromm meant, a practice and discipline of giving of one's own aliveness to another. A person who loves gives "of his joy, of his interest, of his understanding, of his knowledge, of his humor, of his sadness — of all expressions and manifestations of that which is alive in him."[3] I mean generous and disinterested *agape* rather than passionate *eros* or fond *philia*. I mean the love that created the universe, that brings order to chaos and meaning to suffering and causes growth in its proper time. Such a love comes only from a mature adult with integrity, Fromm reminds us. It is not the adoration of a dog or a child.

The books that put heart and breath into me shine with love. I think of A. S. Byatt's *Possession*, devoted to poetry and its scholars; John Crowley's *Little, Big*, infatuated with old houses; Marina and Sergey Dyachenko's *Vita Nostra*, embracing the hammer that shapes us; Karen Russell's *Swamplandia*, a valentine to the Everglades; or Kim Stanley Robinson's *Galileo's Dream*, a serenade to searchers for truth. Terry Pratchett's love is fierce and full of laughter;

---

3. Erich Fromm, *The Art of Loving* (New York: Harper Perennial, 2019), 23.

Mark Twain's is biting and full of laughter; George Eliot's, in *Middlemarch*, shimmers with tears. John Steinbeck loved humanity in its wild, terrible, wonderful variety, as did G. K. Chesterton when he wrote *The Man Who Was Thursday* and Keri Hulme when she wrote *The Bone People*. Because George MacDonald loved a God who loved all, he also loved all. Chiang Yee loved foreign places.[4] For some of them, that love was bitterly fought for, wrested out of darkness, lost, or regained. Nevertheless, in the books they leave us, that love shines and endures.

The books I have mentioned have one thing in common, being in every other respect inimitable. Each one produces the subjective and inward experience I described previously, that orders and renews. I sit down to the banquet that these books spread, and when I rise, I am nourished, satisfied, and changed. After I read such a book, the world shows itself differently to me. It becomes more beautiful, more bearable, more mysterious. I have received a heightened sense of life, of the holiness of all things.

It is almost impossible to find this type of book today. The world is drowning in books that seek only to entertain, to comfort with platitudes, to reassure readers of their own virtue, or to indulge the writer himself. Nor is the trouble isolated to literature. As early as 1989,

---

4. This list is incomplete and could easily be twice as long. Twain's best work, as he himself said, is *Recollections of Joan of Arc*; Steinbeck's is *East of Eden*.

Peter London observed, "Art today seems primarily in the service of decoration, innovation, or self-expression." For him, that kind of art was fraudulent, because it did not pursue the oldest, deepest purposes of art, which are wisdom and communion with the divine.[5] In the same way, writing directed toward self-expression, flattery, and sentimentality is very often a waste of time, and because readers and writers have limited lifetimes, a waste of life as well. More and more often, one can also say similar things about churchgoing and what calls itself Christianity.

The contributing factors to the situation in literature are worth examining in detail, because they illuminate those factors producing shallowness elsewhere. First and foremost, what is clear to the most casual observer is that the relationship between reader and writer has broken down. In recent years, online mobs have accused and hounded author after author, to the point where novels have been withdrawn from publication, sometimes before publication, over bad-faith interpretations of a handful of sentences or, more recently, the choice of a novel's setting.[6] At the same time, both readers and writers have lost much of what is essential to excellence. Readers must be able to

5. Peter London, *No More Secondhand Art: Awakening the Artist Within* (Boston: Shambhala, 1989), 4.
6. See PEN America's *Booklash* report, August 7, 2023, http://pen.org/report /booklash.

read closely and well, to understand what they are reading, and to evaluate a book's level of skill and its relationship to reality. Writers, meanwhile, must be able to live, speak, and write with courage, to accurately observe reality, and to express those observations with clarity, honesty, and a mastery of craft.

Only when the writer has the experience and grace to lead the dance, and when the reader has the experience and grace to follow, in the way that two strangers may clasp hands and waltz for the length of a song, if both know how, does a book of any depth and richness come fully alive. However graceful and skillful the leader, if his partner is deficient, something approximating a waltz may ensue, but unevenly, with much treading on toes. It will not be a true partnership of equals, and it will lack the sensation of flight. If both dancers are deficient, there will be more stumbling than dancing.

A skillful dancer pays attention to her partner's subtle weight shifts, changes in direction and tempo, and the moments of grace and beauty made possible through the coordination and counterbalancing of two bodies. In contrast, someone who gazes at herself in a hand mirror as she waltzes cannot dance well or generously.

Many readers, however, and at least a few writers, are preoccupied with mirror work. Such readers approach books as if they were magic mirrors, not asking for transformation but for reinforcement of preexisting beliefs. Are their opinions echoed, point for point? Are they personally reflected in the book, and if so, are they represented favorably? If they are not made to feel good about themselves or told they are the fairest in the land, these readers feel entitled to punish the author. Having watched a number of witch hunts in various contexts, including the workplace, I suspect that the unconscious defense mechanism of displacement is at play. Rage and frustration at uncontrollable situations or overwhelmingly powerful opponents, whether a war or company executives, that cannot be safely directed at the true cause of that rage, may be displaced onto a weaker, more accessible scapegoat. Sometimes, especially when writers mob other writers, motivations include envy, self-interest, and spite.

Writers, in turn, sometimes construct books like mirrored funhouses, where nothing in the world of the book needs to make sense, be grounded in reality, or persist for longer than the author needs it to. These books do not tell us about the actual world or human experience, only about the writer's passing fancies and narrative necessities, and possess neither solidity nor credibility. Some ideology or other is trumpeted, uncritically upheld by the characters designated as good, and opposed by mustache-twirling villains. Nothing is risked and nothing gained.

At the same time that this is happening, we have collectively forgotten how to talk about books in a rich, nuanced, and meaningful way. As a result of the straitened circumstances of print periodicals, including literary journals and newspapers, a once formidable class of professional critics whose primary work was reading and thinking deeply about books, history, and the world, and whose reputations were built on honesty and good judgment, is all but gone. These critics were as fallible as any other human beings, but the tenor and texture of the conversation about literature was entirely different as a result of their labors. As professional critics retired, many were replaced by underpaid graduate students, freelancers, and authors. The latter group, under the klieg lights of social media, are often anxious to be liked, and as a result, their reviews of books they considered excellent can be nearly indistinguishable from those of books they considered awful.

Outside of periodicals, readers and writers have become acclimated to Amazon's five-star rating system. On Amazon, which distributes over half of all print books sold in the United States,[7] tubs of grout, air filters, and novels of breathtaking brilliance are rated on the same scale, as if these objects were commensurable. But the smallest child who loves fairy tales knows that they are not. To rate a novel in the same crude and casual way that one rates

---

7. A higher estimate of 70–80 percent is given in the August 17, 2020, joint letter to the House Antitrust Subcommittee from the Association of American Publishers, the Authors Guild, and the American Booksellers Association. https://publishers.org/wp-content/uploads/2020/08/Joint-Letter-to-Rep-Cicilline-081720.pdf.

defective poultry shears debases the novel and degrades the conversation about literature. The system is also easily weaponized. A flood of one-star ratings on a tub of grout generally indicates a defective product, but a flood of one-star ratings on a book generally indicates a social-media mobbing.[8]

But I remember a time when we did not rate novels on a five-point scale, or threaten, harangue, and abuse authors and pressure publishers to withdraw their books. I remember when we argued passionately for and against books because of the quality of the prose or the vividness and strangeness of the worlds therein. My friends and I shared books like dreams, like memories we wished to give each other, and we became closer for the exchange. Even now, when I share a meal and a book with others and wage spirited battle over its merits, each of us presenting and defending our generous or ungenerous interpretations, I emerge with a better and deeper appreciation of the book and of the other people present.

We honor books when we discuss them in this way: as art, as gifts, as potential acts of love, rather than as mass-produced factory products. If we are fortunate, the writer has labored to create out of love, out of the wisdom and courage that develop from living with one's eyes open, and with the high level of craft achieved by long study and

---

8. A genuine book, not one generated by AI.

practice. Frequently, however, I notice that those necessary elements are missing.

It has become unfashionable to talk about wisdom, courage, character, and judgment. Worse, the meanings of the words have become muddled and murky, due to the postmodernist preference for performance over substance. The public playacting of these qualities by people severely lacking in them has confused most people and prevented the discernment of the real thing. Yet wisdom, courage, character, and judgment are critical to both writing and living, since by them we strike down roots into that which is imperishable and enduring, and thus add meaning and depth to our writing and our lives. Consider, for example, the following passage from George MacDonald's 1903 novel *Salted with Fire*:

It is folly to suppose that such as follow most the fashions of this world are more enslaved by them than multitudes who follow them only afar off. These reverence the judgments of society in things of far greater importance than the colour or cut of a gown; often without knowing it, they judge life, and truth itself, by the falsest of all measures, namely, the judgment of others falser than themselves; they do not ask what is true or right, but what folk think and say about this or that.[9]

---

9. George MacDonald, *Salted with Fire* (New York: Dodd, Mead, and Company, 1897), 17–18.

One hundred thirty years after publication, MacDonald's criticism of those who judge life and truth not by seeking out what is true and testing it for themselves, but by following others and asking "what folk think and say about this or that," remains as sharp and cogent today as it was when it was written. The insight that he captured and pinned to the page will be recognizable another century hence.

It is now difficult to find writers or Christians who are capable of exercising MacDonald's degree of discernment and judgment, which I call wisdom. Those who have acquired some small amount of wisdom are often afraid to apply it, while those who do not have it tend to avoid the painful lessons through which it is acquired. But mature love joined to wisdom is nothing less than creative power itself, that light whose shining brings order out of chaos and higher life out of life.

In his 1881 novel *Mary Marston*, MacDonald describes a selfish young man, Tom Helmer, from the position of a loving God:

> Like most men, he was so well satisfied with himself, that he saw no occasion to take trouble to be anything better than he was. Never suspecting what a noble creature he was meant to be, he never saw what a poor creature he was.[10]

---

10. George MacDonald, *Mary Marston* (London: Samson Low, Marston, and Company, 1894), 117.

There is no one so good that he might not see a little of himself in these lines, if he is honest, and feel both abashed and beloved. This is because MacDonald put on the power and responsibility of a creator, *the* Creator in fact, relative to his creation, who longs for his creation to realize what he meant it to become.

The loving promise made in this passage is that the author will provide, over the course of the novel, the trials and tribulations that will allow Tom to develop into the honorable man that he could be, if he chooses. Despite Tom's dishonesty and baseness of character, MacDonald will not discard him like refuse, but will go to extraordinary lengths, out of love, to persuade him to grow. In so doing, the author models a higher, holier love. He imparts to the reader the hope, or rather the beginnings of an awareness, that we ourselves might be loved as much as MacDonald loves Tom, even if we have been base and dishonest. It is this awakening that C. S. Lewis refers to when he remarks that MacDonald's writing "shocks us more fully awake than we are for most of our lives."[11] It is this gift of life, freely given, that I mean when I speak of love.

Motivations for reading books vary as widely as human beings do. Some read to escape a monotonous or unbearable life, some to kill time, some because their teachers force them to, some to obtain knowledge or skills, some

---

11. C. S. Lewis, *George MacDonald: An Anthology: 365 Readings* (San Francisco: HarperSanFrancisco, 2001), xxxii.

to be flattered, some to feel. A few read out of hatred. But the highest, truest purpose for reading that I know is given by Annie Dillard, who suggests that when we read, we hope that "the writer will…illuminate and inspire us with wisdom, courage, and the possibility of meaningfulness, and will press upon our minds the deepest mysteries, so we may feel again their majesty and power."[12] Extending her claim further, why do we *live*, if not in hope that some glimpse of deeper meanings, of deeper mysteries, will sometimes flash out through the common moments of our days, and grant us the wisdom and courage to continue living?

To inspire human beings with grace, love, and wisdom— to plant a pale spark in another person's spirit, and breathe upon it, that the soul might quicken to flame—this is and has always been the unspoken, unwritten duty of writers, artists, and God. James Baldwin, paraphrasing a friend, describes the commission in this way: if you are marked as an artist, you bear the responsibility of lightening the darkness in which many, many people live, although those people are strangers, and some may try to kill you.[13] Baldwin's friend was encouraging an actor to play a role he had been avoiding. Baldwin himself was writing to the

---

12. Annie Dillard, *The Writing Life* (New York: Harper Perennial, 2013), 72–73.

13. James Baldwin, "The Artist's Struggle for Integrity," in *The Cross of Redemption: Uncollected Writings*, edited by Randall Kenan (New York: Vintage International, 2010), 55.

body of true artists, who acknowledge their calling and pay the costs. But he might as well have been addressing Christ. In a very real sense, the commission is the same.

The artist's craft is a part of the calling. For writers, craft is the skill with which they express their thought in precise and vivid language, wed meaning to syntax, and give their characters life, distinctness, motion, and motivation. This too has deteriorated in recent years. If a building is constructed from badly rusted girders, the whole structure will totter or collapse outright. So it goes with the books of authors who are lacking in craft.

Paint-by-numbers dialogue may be the most obvious symptom. Listening to any reasonably aware child, one hears, within five minutes, sentences and combinations of words that have never been spoken before. At a very early age, we inherit creative depths we could spend the rest of our lives exploring, and yet we learn to deny that birthright, both our own and others'. Although I might be able to imitate their style, I cannot accurately predict the speech of even those I have known the longest, because each person is as vast as a universe.[14] No matter how much time I spend with someone, that person has private spaces that I will never know. Writing fresh, unexpected, but credible dialogue, which is a long labor of many drafts, means

---

14. Or at least a reasonably complex planetoid.

recognizing this wildness, this hidden creativity, in every human being, including the bit roles and bystanders. Good dialogue is an act of generosity, as well as an expression of faith in human beings. It is exceedingly rare. In much recent fiction and many studio movies, what passes for dialogue is dull and functional, if not clichéd. The latter is particularly deadening. Hearing recycled words in predictable sequences is as inspiring as drinking recycled water and breathing recycled air.

The quality of prose has also suffered. Writers who remember how to mark the stressed and unstressed feet of accentual-syllabic verse are a disappearing species, and venerable if not emeritus. Few writers still chase etymologies through dictionaries and hunt through their paper Roget's thesauruses, opened five ways to five headings, until they strike, at last, the right word in the right place. Some do know the tricks of writing in longhand, or reading drafts aloud to listen for consonance, assonance, repetition, rhyme, and rhythm, adjusting as they go. But even then they may stop before their words are polished to clarity and leaded in place, before the architecture of their syntax is both pleasing and strong. Reading sentences by Peter S. Beagle, or Annie Dillard, one perceives structures both rugged and elegant, each varying from the next, each supporting its meaning and the work as a whole. They last through the years because of their sound construction, much as the ancient dolmans do.

The pressures of the modern world militate against such slow and enduring work. We live in a rush, distracted and off balance, separated from the natural world and the ebb and flow of sunlight, cloistered in glass and concrete, our focus shattered by a monotonically increasing volume of communication. With a handful of exceptions, full-time writers' incomes have dropped precipitously, to a median of $20,300 in 2017 and $20,000 in 2022, even as the cost of living has grown.[15] To eat, stay housed, and obtain healthcare, writers not born to wealth or supported by a spouse either work a day job and scrape writing time from the margins, or deliver manuscripts as quickly as they can. Both conditions reduce opportunities for the concentrated thought, woolgathering, and careful revision that are necessary to produce books of transcendental beauty and lasting value. For similar reasons, fewer and fewer readers have time to read, and those who do have less capacity for difficult books that demand the reader's complete attention.

This deliquescence of concentrated attention is occurring at the same time as vigorous efforts by multiple interest groups to distort and deform language for political gain. George Orwell witnessed the latter during and after his time fighting in the Spanish Civil War,[16] and later dissected

---

15. Authors Guild 2018 and 2023 surveys on writers' incomes.
16. "One of the dreariest effects of this war has been to teach me that the Left-wing press is every bit as spurious and dishonest as that of the Right."

examples in his 1941 essay "Politics and the English Language." As Victor Klemperer and W. H. Auden would also do, Orwell demonstrates how prefabricated phrases cover up incoherent thinking and vicious behavior, including murder, massacre, and nuclear bombing.[17] Only when many individuals put effort into thinking and writing clearly, choosing words not out of reflexive habit but out of a desire to precisely and accurately express their thoughts, will a society be capable of facing and dealing with reality.

Language is the narrow rope bridge with which we traverse the vast abysses between two people, or two cultures, or two times. When it is twisted and frayed for political purposes, those chasms become uncrossable; friendship recedes into estrangement; both familial and institutional relationships snap. Literature, having no firm footing, must cling and crawl, and cannot stand to full height. As Orwell, Klemperer, and Auden noted, in such confusion, evil passes unremarked.

Given the circumstances, the writer who holds fast to a vision of the real and sets stone upon stone, word upon

---

George Orwell, *Homage to Catalonia* (Boston: Mariner Books, 2015), 215.

17. George Orwell, "Politics and the English Language," *Horizon* 13, no. 76 (April 1946): 252–265. https://www.orwellfoundation.com/the -orwell-foundation/orwell/essays-and-other-works/politics-and-the-english -language. See also Victor Klemperer, *The Language of the Third Reich*, trans. Martin Brady (London: Bloomsbury, 2013), 15, and W. H. Auden, "Words and the Word," in *Secondary Worlds* (New York: Random House, 1968), 127–128.

word, until she has built a shelter both sturdy and satisfying, not for herself but for the rest of the world, is an
absolute fool. So are the worker bees in my hive, who construct, flake by secreted flake, waxen galleries of comb,
then fill them with distilled nectars from a million flowers. They do this for the sake of unborn generations, deriving little personal benefit, since a summer worker lives
no more than seven weeks before dying of exhaustion.
But only through such loving labors can the hive survive
the winter, feeding on the sweetness gathered and concentrated by those who went before. Only through such
a labor can the artist bring light into the darkness of the
world. And so we hurl ourselves toward the flowers, the
stones, the words.

Faith of a sort is necessary, if only faith in humanity,
in a future, in the thin white hyphens of unhatched possibility anchored in their cells. Nevertheless, many of the
writers I have named and will name in this book, including MacDonald, Dillard, Miłosz, Auden, and Baldwin,
also acknowledge some personal experience of God, of
One who surpasses understanding, whose presence is mystery and grace. I think this no coincidence. A life and a
literature that does not allow space for the possibility of
such a One — at this moment I am not speaking of a single belief, Christian or otherwise, but of an openness to
something greater than the self — can never exceed human
dimensions. And given the false and brittle conceptions

that result from deifying the human mind, the result is frequently even less.

Literature, as I have mentioned, is a specific instance of a general problem. Those qualities that I have described as both vanishing and vital, including love, wisdom, grace, and light, are not only what the reader seeks in literature, however unconsciously, but also what the Christian pursues in her walk with God. At the same time that those qualities are waning in book publishing, they are waning in many churches across the world, regardless of denomination. What else but this absence can explain the dogmatic schisms, the sexual predators, the hypocrisies and vanities proclaimed at the pulpit, the dwindling congregations, and the dry and arid lives of so many churchgoers and parishioners?

I left a nondenominational church after a leader in another state boasted that COVID-19 had been God's answer to his prayers for punishment, and none of the elders in my church, though they loved God, would gainsay him. I listened to a sermon in a Baptist church where the preacher raved against the wickedness of a hypochondriac woman who had inscribed "I told you I was sick" on her gravestone, when I had always found that line, which is on William H. Hahn Jr.'s stone in Princeton Cemetery, to be hilarious.[18] I was grabbed from behind for an

---

18. Other gravestones with this joke include those of B. P. Roberts, who was probably the woman the preacher had in mind, and Spike Milligan, where the line is engraved in Gaelic.

unwanted massage by an elder in a Presbyterian church, who then argued that because he had only done so once in three years, rather than four or five times, I should not be angry with him. And I have watched Catholic, Evangelical, and Eastern Orthodox men in my workplace gleefully accusing women who had abortions of murder, and ordering me to humble myself when I disputed their accusations.[19]

The problem is not new, because human nature is not new, but we have forgotten many old and worthy ways of addressing it. This should not be the case. More hopefully put, this does not have to remain the case. I would be far more discouraged if I had not also known Christians in many countries, of various denominations, whose walk in Christ is deep and true, and a God whose love is an ordering white flame, and books written by the light of that flame. Because I have encountered these things, I know they are possible, and I know a little of their inestimable worth.

My point is that, for many readers, as well as for many Christians, what is on offer in recent years of book publishing and church life is, in the main, lifeless, without love, without hope, without mystery. In 1994, Sven

---

19. To be clear, the fault does not lie in Christianity—Christians have not treated me worse than those who are not Christian—but in human nature. My point is that many who call themselves Christians and hold positions of responsibility in churches nevertheless lack Christ, and remain in the world and of it.

Birkerts predicted that corporate media and online networks would flatten and homogenize human life, eradicating depth, privacy, and individual subjectivity. His fear was that humanity would grow shallower, turning away from depth and wisdom toward "the ersatz security of a vast lateral connectedness."[20] That fear was prescient. We now live in the flattened, interconnected future that Birkerts foresaw, with the corresponding losses of wisdom, love, depth, and grace. Often, the truth is lost as well.

Because these changes and their causes are societal and structural rather than individual, they may seem as immovable and unchanging as mountains. But I believe restoration is possible, and that it must happen individually, if it will happen at all. It will be the responsibility of individual readers and writers, artists and Christians, to recover what has been lost, to remember what is of highest importance, and to coax dying embers to flame, that we might again catch fire and burn to life.

20. Sven Birkerts, *The Gutenberg Elegies: The Fate of Reading in an Electronic Age* (New York: Faber and Faber, 2006), 228.

Chapter Two

READING BADLY,
READING WELL

W<small>HAT</small> I <small>HAVE LEARNED OVER THE YEARS, BY ACCI-</small>
dent and not as part of any curriculum, is that, at
its best, given the right book at the right moment, reading
is an encounter with what is timeless. Opening a book, we
sink into a separate place in our own being, sometimes so
deeply that the concrete world fades from our perception.
Black text on a white page becomes music, color, texture,
movement, voices, flavors, monsters, wonders, no less vivid
for being intangible. If the time is right, if the author has

mastered the craft and herself, if she gives out of her own aliveness, something of the eternal touches us there, in that place that is no place at all. Our fingers grasp the hem of a robe, or an angel's hand brushes against our hip, and we are healed or stricken, changed utterly.

Books are not the only form of art that can transfigure us. Certain pieces of music, sculpture, theater, or dance, done honestly and well, have also operated upon me in this way. When I finished *Chrono Trigger*, two decades after everyone else, I went outside with unshed tears in my eyes and saw the bluest sky I can remember.

Nevertheless, I have been remade more often by books than by other art forms. This may be because the vast majority of books are, in the end, authored by one person, and therefore subject to fewer external pressures, falsifications, and misinterpretations than work that must pass through the hands of producers, performers, and record label and film executives to reach the wider world. If the artist has achieved a singular vision, and opened a window upon eternity, that vision may encounter fewer obstacles in its journey toward us, and have a better chance of arriving intact, if it takes the shape of a book.[1]

---

1. Cf. T. S. Eliot, "The Possibility of a Poetic Drama," in *The Sacred Wood* (New York: Knopf, 1921), 62: "The intervention of performers introduces a complication of economic conditions which is in itself likely to be injurious. A struggle, more or less unconscious, between the creator and the interpreter is almost inevitable. The interest of a performer is almost certain to be centred in himself: a very slight acquaintance with actors and musicians will

But even if the vision is perfectly transmitted, the reader can be unable or unwilling to receive it.

In the ordinary course of education, we are not, any of us, really taught to read, not the Bible, not novels, not nonfiction or poetry, just as none of us are really taught to live. By this I mean neither bare literacy, which is the decoding of letters and glyphs on road signs and hospital forms, nor bare life, which is the minimal survival of an animal in a given environment. A few people stumble into the depths of reading or living, here and there, through desperation, observation, or guidance from those further along the path. But for the most part we are dragged through the alphabet, vocabulary lists, a few grammar rules, sentence diagrams if we are lucky, and a set of books we must boil down to five-paragraph essays on symbolism, some simplified moral or message, and presumptuous claims about the author's intent. Then we are released like so many wolves into the wild.

We are, in short, taught to look for easy answers, to dismiss ambiguity and mystery, to stomp with closed mind and steel-toed boots over a living bed of emerald moss, and to make confident assertions about what we do not understand. We are not taught how to recognize art that is powerful, enduring, or sacred, or how to approach it in such a way that it can come to change our lives.

---

testify. The performer is interested not in form but in opportunities for virtuosity or in the communication of his 'personality'..."

Rachel Held Evans reminds us that after God came into the world as a human being, most of Jesus' ministry was spent telling stories, so many that, according to Matthew 13:34, "he did not say anything to [the crowds] without using a parable" (NIV).[2] One might say that He told such radical and perplexing parables in order to shock the hearer into coming fully alive. Amy-Jill Levine says of the parables that we should be "thinking less about what they 'mean,' and more about what they can 'do': remind, provoke, refine, confront, disturb."[3] If we follow her suggestion to encounter those stories in the fullness of our being, in open inquiry, and without foregone conclusions, then we find ourselves directed toward better and more generous readings of all works of literature, biblical and otherwise. What does a novel do to us? How does it remind, provoke, refine, confront, and disturb us, and how do we live differently afterward? No single moral can be extracted from a good book without killing whatever was lively and multiplicitous and bright within it, just as no one has declared the one true meaning of any of Jesus' parables without opening his hands to find, where something had been warm and fluttering, a cold dead mass.

---

2. Rachel Held Evans, *Inspired: Slaying Giants, Walking on Water, and Loving the Bible Again* (Nashville: Nelson Books, 2018), 158.

3. Amy-Jill Levine, *Short Stories by Jesus: The Enigmatic Parables of a Controversial Rabbi* (New York: HarperOne, 2014), 4, also quoted in Evans, *Inspired*.

The desire to substitute one simple meaning or interpretation for an intractably complex text is a very old one. In 1867, George MacDonald was already fending off readers who insisted that he tell them the meaning of each story, responding: "A genuine work of art must mean many things; the truer its art, the more things it will mean."[4] He compared his readers' demands for explanations to a demand that he boil roses. He had given them the story itself, the living thing, with its fragrance and thorns, but he would not help them turn either stories or roses into dead and lifeless pulp.

In 2002, queer theorist Eve Sedgwick described a dominant trend in queer criticism that she called "paranoid reading," an outgrowth of the hermeneutics of suspicion, that begins by assuming that every text reproduces or perpetuates oppression, preemptively condemns it, and afterward gathers selective evidence to uphold that condemnation. The result is a kind of tautological thinking that "masquerad[es] as the stuff of truth," and is now threatening to become the only acceptable mode of critical analysis.[5] Paranoid reading has served as the pretext for multiple attacks on authors, many of them unjustified. What is curious is that this secular mode of criticism has

---

4. George MacDonald, "The Fantastic Imagination," in *A Dish of Orts* (London: Samson Low, Marston & Company, 1895), 317.
5. Eve Kosofsky Sedgwick, "Paranoid Reading, Reparative Reading," in *Touching Feeling* (Durham, NC: Duke University Press, 2002), 123–151.

religious parallels, namely in those Christians who apply the Bible like a set of HOA covenants, eagerly measuring the height of their neighbors' grass and informing them of millimeter infractions.

Another small-minded method of reading is the grading of texts with strict rubric in hand, giving points for conformity to arbitrary rules and deducting for nonconformity. Nonconformity, of course, circumscribes both originality and innovation, and most authors are not schoolchildren learning to write, but this does not appear to discourage the graders. To give one example, many a literary Procrustes has turned the present classification of genres into an iron bed. Modern genres are marketing categories developed for the convenience of booksellers, helping them to sort through the hundreds of thousands of titles published annually and to match consumers with products they are likely to buy. But readers have mistaken these recently created sales labels for an ahistorical taxonomy valuable in and of itself. A century ago, fiction was divided into novels, sometimes serialized, and collections of stories. Bookstores did not label their wares as science fiction, mystery, young adult, and African American, that oddest of categories. Those books were no less capable of greatness for that.

Arguing over books that fail to fit neatly into one marketing category or another, as though the borders of genre were the Durand Line and Radcliffe Line and the

McMahon Line, rather than useful tools for marketers, booksellers, and a subset of scholars, has always struck me as a pointless exercise. Strict categories, rules, rubrics, and boxes can provide a sense of safety and security, and in an increasingly unstable and chaotic world, people long for the sense of safety that such rubrics and boxes provide, as well as their ability to save us the strain of thinking.[6] We forget that this is, ultimately, the allure of authoritarianism, and that art and life do not flourish in cages. No book of lasting worth, and no richly lived life, will abide by commercial or stereotypical constraints. When we try to force people and books into too-small boxes, at worst we do violence, and at best we are likely to miss the bright shadow and beating wings of the spirit that flies over us and away.

Another naïve form of reading demands that badly behaving characters must be punished and well-behaved ones rewarded. When a book does not follow the just world fallacy, and instead depicts the real injustices that often persist without remedy, this kind of reader protests. It is a child's protest, uttered by the child self, and understandable.[7] Nevertheless, it is regrettable when an adult

---

6. To avoid misunderstanding, I am not referring to rules that prevent predictable physical harm to vulnerable populations, that are based in reality and a wise understanding of human behavior.

7. G. K. Chesterton once took children to see a Maurice Maeterlinck play and wrote about their dissatisfaction with the lack of punishment for the wicked and reward for the good. His alternative, more generous explanation:

has lived a life so wrapped in cotton wool that he has no awareness of the cruelty and unfairness in human beings and human society, or the cruelty and unfairness of life itself. He has had no real encounter with the wolves that tear apart living deer, the parasitical wasp that lays its eggs in a caterpillar, or the cross where a man hung in terror and pain for six hours before dying, guilty only of speaking the truth. He has not read Ecclesiastes 8:14, which reminds us that "there are righteous people to whom it happens according to the deeds of the wicked, and there are wicked people to whom it happens according to the deeds of the righteous." He does not know that in many cases justice must wait for God's final administration. People unfamiliar with the harshness of the world are like porcelain carefully packed and handled with the greatest gentleness to avoid chips and scratches. Their reading reflects their inexperience.

If and when this type of reader claims that the author who does not deliver poetic justice condones his characters' misbehavior, that reader has progressed from sentimentality to smear. Such a reading inevitably concludes in a declaration of the author's immorality and condemnation of the work. For both critical theorists practicing paranoid reading and would-be religious inquisitors, books must be morally

---

"For children are innocent and love justice; while most of us are wicked and naturally prefer mercy." "On Household Gods and Goblins," *New Witness* 20, no. 517 (October 6, 1922), 213.

irreproachable, or else burned. In the United States, this particular approach to literature has held sway since the passage of the federal Comstock Act in 1873.

In 1917, H. L. Mencken examined this distinctly American mode of reading, calling it Puritanism for its historical roots:

> The American, try as he will, can never imagine any work of the imagination as wholly devoid of moral content. It must either tend toward the promotion of virtue, or be suspect and abominable....
>
> A novel or a play is judged among us, not by its dignity of conception, its artistic honesty, its perfection of workmanship, but almost entirely by its orthodoxy of doctrine, its platitudinousness, its usefulness as a moral tract....
>
> The Puritan's utter lack of aesthetic sense, his distrust of all romantic emotion, his unmatchable intolerance of opposition, his unbreakable belief in his own bleak and narrow views, his savage cruelty of attack, his lust for relentless and barbarous persecution — these things have put an almost unbearable burden upon the exchange of ideas in the United States.[8]

The Puritan insistence on black-and-white morality in art and literature, Mencken notes, has hindered the

8. H. L. Mencken, "Puritanism as a Literary Force," in *A Book of Prefaces*, 2nd ed. (New York: Knopf, 1918), 200–202.

development of both art and literature in the United States, not least through the promulgation and enforcement of the state and federal Comstock Acts. Those laws banned the mailing of pornography, as well as a wide variety of texts Anthony Comstock deemed indecent, including the *Decameron*, the *Arabian Nights*, *Lysistrata*, *The Canterbury Tales*, *Leaves of Grass*, and novels by Thomas Hardy, Émile Zola, Ernest Hemingway, John Steinbeck, William Faulkner, F. Scott Fitzgerald, James Joyce, D. H. Lawrence, Victor Hugo, and Oscar Wilde; contraceptives; and educational materials on contraceptives. Art gallery owners, publishers, nurses, and feminists were prosecuted and sentenced to heavy fines and hard labor. In 1872, Comstock arrested George Francis Train for reprinting parts of the Old Testament in serial form. In 1895, J. B. Wise from Clay Center, Kansas, was found guilty of mailing obscene material and fined $50 for sending a postcard with Isaiah 12:36.[9]

Publishers began inserting morality clauses in their writers' contracts in response to the Comstock laws, displacing legal liability onto the writer. The 1914 contract for Theodore Dreiser's *The Genius*, published by John Lane Co., included the line "The author hereby guarantees... that the work... contains nothing of a sensitive, an

---

9. Mentioned in Mencken, *A Book of Prefaces*, 261 and elaborated upon in Hal D. Sears, *The Sex Radicals: Free Love in High Victorian America* (Lawrence: University Press of Kansas, 1977), 107.

immoral or a libelous nature." These morality clauses not only persist today but have been dramatically expanded, requiring not only the book but the author to be morally unimpeachable. Had Dreiser signed his contract one hundred ten years later, it might also have included a clause, as the contract for this book does, allowing his publisher to withdraw the book from publication in case of a "Conduct Incident" defined as the "widespread public condemnation of Author" due to "highly offensive behavior."

Two years after publication of *The Genius*, after the book had sold eight thousand copies, the New York Society for the Suppression of Vice threatened to prosecute the publisher if the book was not withdrawn. The publisher promptly withdrew it.[10] Though he did not consider *The Genius* to be a good book, Mencken observed that the "professional book-baiters" who attacked Dreiser benefited from sympathetic laws and courts, newspapers that printed their inflammatory accusations prior to the trial, "far more money than any writer could hope to muster" at their disposal, and the fear and envy of other writers. "When an author is attacked," he noted, "a good many of his rivals see only a personal benefit in his difficulties, and not a menace to the whole order, and a good many others are afraid to go to his aid because of the danger of bringing down the moralists' rage upon

---

10. Mencken, *A Book of Prefaces*, 270 n. 1.

themselves."[11] That atmosphere of fear and cowardice, envy and power-seeking, produced a mawkish, artificial literature completely unrelated to life as it was lived. Himself a magazine editor, Mencken describes turning down excellent work that would have been published immediately in Europe, for fear of those readers who would report him to the police, because he could not bear the expense of having his office raided and forthcoming issues of his magazine seized.[12] Dreiser was fortunate. A beneficiary paid for his legal expenses. He sued his publisher and won.

It goes without saying, for anyone paying attention, that many publishers, writers, and Puritan crusaders today behave much as they did a hundred years ago, though the religious element has been replaced by various secular articles of faith.[13] Publishers have recently bowdlerized *Huck Finn*, Roald Dahl's books, and Ursula K. Le Guin's *Catwings* series, the latter for using words like *dumb*. Twitter serves as a modern-day Society for the Suppression of Vice. The majority of books that survive in this environment

---

11. Mencken, *A Book of Prefaces*, 271–272.

12. Mencken, 277–278.

13. For the blessedly unaware, see, in addition to the incidents described in PEN America's *Booklash* report, the cancellation of book contracts for Gillian Philip and Blaine Pardoe; the withdrawal of an award nomination for Lauren Hough for suggesting that people read her mobbed friend's book before criticizing it; and the yearslong campaign of death and rape threats against J. K. Rowling.

display the very same flaws of mawkishness and artificiality that Mencken remarked a hundred years ago.

Today, the federal Comstock Act remains on the books, although the portion related to contraception was struck down as unconstitutional in *Griswold v. Connecticut* in 1965 and *Eisenstadt v. Baird* in 1972. The act was updated in 1994 to increase the fine from $5,000 to $250,000, and again in 1996 to apply to the internet, notably over the protests of Congresswoman Patricia Schroeder, who later became president and CEO of the Association of American Publishers.[14] While the act has not been actively enforced in decades, activists in Texas revived it for their lawsuit against mifepristone, and US District Judge Matthew J. Kacsmaryk cited the Act over a dozen times in his April 2023 ruling. The Supreme Court is expected to issue their decision around the time of this book's publication. The Puritan mode of reading, meanwhile, continues to be practiced and enforced by readers of all stripes. With the spread of social media, it has become a major cultural export.

One could infer from Mencken's essay that in the United States, and perhaps in several other countries as well, the practice of reading literature has never been cleanly severed from the practice of reading the Bible; that until recent decades, readers of one tended to be readers of the

---

14. See Pat Schroeder's September 24, 1996, congressional floor speech, "Comstock Act Still on the Books," delivered to the US House of Representatives, Washington, DC, http://gos.sbc.edu/s/schroeder.html.

other; and that readers are frequently bad at reading both. As a consequence, literary analysis as practiced in American institutions has never been fully separated from either biblical exegesis or Puritan thought, except in the most superficial aspects. A significant number of American and Americanized readers, critics, and academics who declare explicitly secular modes of inquiry, whether Freudian, postmodernist, Marxist, feminist, or queer, and choose secular texts to dissect are still pulled along by the unacknowledged undertow of Puritanism. This becomes apparent when they end up dividing authors and books into the elect and the damned, proclaiming this or that path to the salvation of the soul, and imposing orthodoxies and punishing heresies.

All appearances to the contrary, that entanglement offers a glint of hope. Given how closely biblical and literary readings are entwined, if we learn to cultivate a wholehearted approach to either, holding out open hands to the Good Book or any good book and receiving whatever light is given in that moment, then we might also extend such graciousness to the other. As far as I am concerned, it does not matter whether the reader begins to read redemptively with the Bible or with literature. The important thing is that she does begin.

⟳

Although I know the power, vitality, and grace of certain books and works of art and literature, I do not think that books as a whole will save us. Several years ago, I was on a panel of authors assembled to speak before librarians. The last question, as I recall, was whether we thought fiction was a force for good. Of course it was, the first author said, because fiction engendered empathy. One after another, the other five authors agreed.

I dissented. Storytelling, I said, is a natural human impulse, like humming, singing, or dancing, that children in any country will do without encouragement. Like humming, singing, or dancing, however, it is not inherently good. One can sing nationalistic songs, like the Horst Wessel Lied, in order to terrorize, or dance for the head of John the Baptist on a platter. Plenty of stories are told in order to diminish and denigrate, to harm and to dehumanize, as I know from experience.

If readers claim that reading increases empathy, and that empathy is unquestionably good, then they can justify their choice of pastime as moral and consider themselves more virtuous than others. If writers make that claim, they can frame their historically disreputable profession as altruistic, even angelic, whether or not they write with love, skill, and wisdom. The claim that reading is a moral act because it produces empathy is so common and accepted nowadays that most people do not stop to wonder why, exactly, reading must be morally justified, unlike singing, dancing, drawing, driving, golfing, diving, or climbing Mount Everest. Mencken's diagnosis of metastasized Puritanism in American literature may be the answer.

The unqualified assertion that reading results in empathy, or the active and inward experience of another person's feelings, and that therefore reading is virtuous, is a product of the twenty-first century.[15] The word *empathy* itself was only coined in 1908, as a translation of German *Einfühlung*, and the word did not become popular until the 1980s. In contrast, *compassion*, which refers to "feeling with" or "feeling for" another person, rather than empathy's "feeling as" or "feeling in," has been in wide use since 1350.[16] The critical distinction between empathy and compassion is that compassion does not involve projective identification with another person. The compassionate human being experiences her own distinct emotions, separate from anyone else's, and thus is not controlled or manipulated by others, but free to act with wisdom and detachment.

In *The Moral Laboratory*, published in 2000, Jèmeljan Hakemulder reviews fifty-four studies on the relationship between reading, empathy, and moral development, finding subtle and nuanced results that raise more questions than they answer.[17] In one 1988 study, students encour-

---

15. To see the spike in interest after 2000, search for *reading * empathy* on Google Ngram Viewer, at books.google.com/ngrams.
16. Edwin Friedman, *A Failure of Nerve: Leadership in the Age of the Quick Fix* (New York: Seabury, 2007), 134–135. His observation can be confirmed with Google Ngram Viewer.
17. Where language barriers or difficulties in obtaining full-length dissertations existed, the descriptions of the following studies rely on Hakemulder's

aged to take an empathetic, affective approach to morally ambiguous World War II narratives expressed more vengefulness toward certain characters than those encouraged to take a cognitive approach.[18] One 1975 dissertation found that reading could move subjects' average moral development from the second to third stage of the six-stage Kohlberg moral development scale: that is, from self-interest to people-pleasing.[19] Other studies suggested that readers expressed greater empathy for characters coded as good than for characters coded as bad,[20] and for characters who shared the reader's experiences, whether that was pregnancy or a common cultural background.[21] A 1991 dissertation observed that while narratives could increase empathy among preschoolers, that increase in empathy

---

literature review. See Jèmeljan Hakemulder, *The Moral Laboratory* (Amsterdam: John Benjamins, 2000), 53–74.

18. Dick Schram and Cor Geljon, "Effecten van affectieve en cognitieve lesmethoden op de receptie van verhalen over de Tweede Wereldoorlog," *Spiegel* 6, no. 3 (1988): 321–335.

19. Donald Richard Keefe, "A Comparison of the Effect of Teacher and Student Led Discussions of Short Stories and Case Accounts on the Moral Reasoning of Adolescents Using the Kohlberg Model," PhD diss., University of Illinois, Urbana-Champaign, 1975. Note that moral reasoning at the level of universal human rights does not occur until Kohlberg's sixth stage.

20. Paul E. Jose and William F. Brewer, "Development of Story Liking: Character Identification, Suspense, and Outcome Resolution," *Developmental Psychology* 20 (1984): 911–924.

21. Hakemulder, 71–72, and Steen F. Larsen and János László, "Cultural-Historical Knowledge and Personal Experience in Appreciation of Literature," *European Journal of Social Psychology* 20 (1990): 425–440.

did not translate to an increase in altruistic behavior.[22] All studies were designed to explore short-term effects only, and so persistence of any of the effects is unknown.

Researchers were cautious about their mixed findings. In contrast, Lynn Hunt's *The Invention of Human Rights*, published in 2002, advanced the unequivocal claim that reading novels increases readers' empathy, and that the empathy of readers produced a distinct moral good: the recognition of universal human rights. Specifically, she proposes that popular early English and French novels, especially Samuel Richardson's *Pamela* (1740) and *Clarissa* (1748) and Jean-Jacques Rousseau's *Julie* (1761), by teaching readers to empathize with the female protagonists, led directly to the 1776 American Declaration of Independence and the 1789 French Declaration of the Rights of Man and of the Citizen. For Hunt, human rights are based in empathy, that is, our ability to feel other people's emotions and to project ourselves into others to the point of identifying with them.[23] Prior to these novels, she says, the average person did not realize that other people could feel emotions and suffer as well. Because empathy is a twentieth-century coinage, Hunt deliberately conflates it

---

22. Lori Sandford Wiley, "Impact of Story-Based and Problem-Solving Character Education on Altruistic Behavior in the Preschool Classroom," PhD diss., Boston College, 1991.

23. Lynn Hunt, *Inventing Human Rights: A History* (New York: W. W. Norton, 2007), 55.

with compassion and sympathy, although these words are distinct in meaning.[24]

While the argument is, on the surface, an attractive one, it falls apart when considered closely. The book relies upon the post hoc ergo propter hoc fallacy,[25] assuming that because two declarations asserting human rights occurred in the decades after the aforementioned novels were published, one must have caused the other. No compelling reason is given for why readers' empathy should be considered the primary factor, rather than concurrent geopolitical or economic tensions or increasing rates of literacy, which allowed for the swift spread of ideas. Hunt also overlooks John Lilburne's agitation in the 1640s for "freeborn rights," which included no imprisonment without due process, trial by a jury of peers, and equality of all

---

24. It is never clear what Hunt means by *empathy*, as the word takes on different definitions throughout the book, and is used interchangeably with *sympathy* and *compassion*. At one point *empathy* is defined as the "recognition that others have minds like your own," which is more properly called theory of mind. *Clarissa* is described as stimulating "empathy or compassion" that made readers "more sympathetic toward others...and therefore more moral." A little later on, Hunt declares that she is substituting the word *empathy* for eighteenth-century occurrences of the word *sympathy*. Hunt, *Inventing Human Rights*, 33, 54, 64–65.

25. "After this, therefore because of this." Hunt's own words: "Can it be coincidental that the three greatest novels of psychological identification of the eighteenth century...were all published in the period that immediately preceded the appearance of the concept of 'the rights of man'?" My answer is yes. Hunt, *Inventing Human Rights*, 39.

before the law, a more plausible antecedent of the declarations than *Pamela*.

What is most perplexing is how Hunt describes readers' passionate and tearful identification with the female protagonists of *Pamela*, *Clarissa*, and *Julie*, claims that this act of identifying with others led to the establishment of basic human rights, and then admits that women were omitted from the two declarations of rights supposed to result from the popularity of those novels. Women in the United States and France only received the rights of full citizens one hundred and fifty years after those declarations, two hundred years after the publications of those novels. Either one attributes the eventual recognition of women's human rights to two male novelists from the eighteenth century, rather than the many women and sympathetic men who fought for women's rights, or else Hunt's syllogistic claim that reading leads to empathy with those unlike oneself, that empathy causes the recognition of others' human rights, and that therefore reading is a moral act, does not hold.

Though my disagreement with Hunt may seem academic, her book was highly influential, and its claims have led to a serious misapprehension of the uses of the story and the value of empathy, which is repeated not only by readers and writers but also by pastors in pulpits. Our willingness to recognize other people's human rights must not be based upon transient and subjective emotions aroused by storytelling, because storytelling is just as capable of arousing fear, rage, and hatred toward individuals and groups, and cutting off our awareness of others' humanity, as it is capable of doing the opposite. The recognition, codification, and protection of human rights must instead be based upon wisdom, justice, and fairness, which are not altered by changes in emotional valence.

A more fundamental mistake is seeing empathy as a positive virtue, rather than a neutral, useful skill. As rabbi and therapist Edwin Friedman wrote in *A Failure of Nerve*, originally published in 1997, prioritizing empathy over responsibility and integrity creates leaders who are unable to set limits on other people's behavior or make hard decisions because they are reluctant to let others feel any discomfort or pain. Discomfort and pain are unavoidable in life and can lead to growth and the setting of healthy limits. But if we project ourselves into another person to the point of experiencing his feelings as our own, we may try to protect him from discomfort and pain in order to protect ourselves, and thereby stunt his growth or ignore or enable his evil behavior. Friedman argues that empathy distracts us from real destructiveness, which always exhibits "the un-self-regulating invasiveness of another's space" and is "utterly unresponsive to empathy."[26]

Empathy also makes us vulnerable to manipulation by immature, unscrupulous, or authoritarian actors who

---

26. Friedman, *A Failure of Nerve*, 134.

can entangle us in a convincing performance of emotions. Sarah Schulman has observed that both entitled and traumatized people frequently experience disproportionate emotional reactions to stimuli in the present moment. If we empathize with them, taking their excessive emotions as our own, we may join them in controlling or unjustly punishing others on the basis of feelings rather than fact. Schulman writes: "It may even be considered victimizing by the supremacist/traumatized person to not simply follow their orders when they 'feel' or say that they 'feel' endangered, even if that feeling is retrospective."[27] As with human rights, when judgment and punishment are based on subjective feelings rather than factual reality, the outcome is appalling injustice.

Storytelling can also lead us to believe untrue things. In a 2013 study, P. Matthijs Bal and Martijn Veltkamp found that false statements in fictional narratives had an increasing influence on readers over time.[28] The problem is larger than single false statements, however, because all fiction is, at bottom, fabrication. Depending on the context and the storyteller's motives, whether conscious or unconscious,

---

27. Sarah Schulman, *Conflict Is Not Abuse: Overstating Harm, Community Responsibility, and the Duty of Repair* (Vancouver, BC: Arsenal Pulp Press, 2016), 154.
28. P. Matthijs Bal and Martijn Veltkamp, "How Does Fiction Reading Influence Empathy? An Experimental Investigation on the Role of Emotional Transportation," *PLOS ONE* 8, no. 1 (January 30, 2013): e55341, DOI: 10.1371/journal.pone.0055341.

fiction can unveil to us truths we have refused to see, or it can deliver propaganda, gossip, slander, conspiracy theories, disinformation, and other things injurious to truth. It is a tool for persuasion and influence, and like any other tool can be used for good and ill.

In Botticelli's *Calumny of Apelles*, which hangs in the Uffizi Gallery, hardly anyone glances at the naked, silent figure of Truth, while Calumny, dragging her victim by the hair, surrounded by supporters, receives a full hearing from the king. According to Lucian of Samosata, a jealous professional rival once falsely accused the painter Apelles of involvement in a conspiracy. Apelles was sentenced to death, but released after one of the conspirators affirmed his innocence. Once freed, Apelles painted an allegory of the event. Only Lucian's description of that painting survives, but Botticelli relied upon that description for his recreation of Apelles' painting. The *Calumny* serves as a portrait of the lowest forms of storytelling. "We all delight in whispering and insinuations," Lucian wrote in the second century. "I know people whose ears are as agreeably titillated with slander as their skin with a feather."[29]

We all know, and sometimes are, such people. At a recent wedding, the guest seated beside me asked if I had met a certain writer. I had. He asked what she was like, and I said that I could not infer much from a brief

---

29. Lucian, "Slander, a Warning," in *The Works of Lucian of Samosata*, trans. H. W. Fowler and F. G. Fowler, vol. 4 (Oxford, UK: Clarendon, 1905), 9.

encounter. He expressed disappointment, saying he had wanted me to give him "dirt" on her. In the present decade, as it was in Lucian's time, his prurient curiosity is not uncommon. Those who share it give license to informers, tabloid reporters, liars, and the like. Most middle school girls know the power of a story told first, or told with some scandalous detail, however false. Rarely does that kind of story ennoble life, or allow two human beings to see each other and be seen in their wholeness, or do honor and justice to God or God's creation. Fiction is capable of the same degradation.

My intention is not to discourage reading, nor to denigrate it. At the very least, time spent reading is time not spent on dangerous, criminal, or chemical recreations. But I believe that reading is far more complicated than the popular conception of it, and that repeating false claims about its moral goodness can obscure both its finer and baser qualities. Neither literature nor human beings can flourish when readers and writers are required to be both paragons of virtue and vicious enforcers of constantly changing moral codes. The reader who can say "I read novels because I enjoy them, and because they help me find meaning in my life," or "I read novels because they are entertaining and pass the time," rather than "I read because it is virtuous to do so, and it makes me a better person," has freed herself from the prison of literary Puritanism. In so doing, she leaves the door open to other jailbreaks as well.

Reading should not be confused with cultivating integrity, which is far harder. A university lecturer once suggested to me that people would be better and kinder if they read more books. If this were true, literature departments and publishing companies would be earthly representations of heaven. This is not and has never been the case. Furthermore, many illiterate people throughout history have lived brave, generous, holy lives, Joan of Arc for one, and the world is better for the light they brought into it. Readers who assume that reading alone will improve one's character will neglect what actually does: integrating pain, struggle, failure, and regret into our lives and selves and thus becoming whole and wholly aware.[30]

Hannah Arendt reminds us that many officials in the Third Reich adored Bach and Hölderlin. They read literature and appreciated the arts while murdering millions. As she points out, reading, listening to music, and viewing paintings have "nothing whatever to do with thought, which, as we must remember, is an *activity* and not the passive enjoyment of something."[31] For Arendt, only someone who has planted deep roots in critical thought and remembrance of the past can withstand the kind of rootless evil that now and then sweeps over the world. To

---

30. *Whole* and *holy* share an etymological root.
31. Hannah Arendt, *Responsibility and Judgment* (New York: Schocken Books, 2003), 97.

those two prophylactics I would add a third, that of "being rooted and grounded in love" (Eph. 3:17).

Reading will not save us. Books will not save us, except for the very few that teach us to hunger for wisdom and truth. This is not to dismiss the reading of books for pleasure. Pleasure is necessary; it eases our burdens and lightens our days. But restricting one's reading to books that seek only to entertain, that do not demand more and give more, that do not convict, transform, or challenge the reader, is not far removed from living a life dissipated in other pleasures and entertainments. It is to starve oneself of what is essential. It is a refusal to grow.

In recent decades, the dominant paradigm for storytelling has been that of television and movies, where little is asked of the audience, while everything is demanded of cast and crew, writers and directors, production and postproduction staff. Special-effects artists sweat over explosions and the simulated physics of corkscrew curls. Sound engineers snowshoe up mountains to record Foley effects. Costume, makeup, and set designers whip up stunning visual confections and seamless prostheses. Actors psychoanalyze, interpret, and inhabit their roles, and deliver dialogue written by roomfuls of writers. The moviegoer provides only payment, if that, and passively consumes what is served through the screen. At no point is he required to compose music, imagine landscapes and faces, conjure up tastes, smells, and textures, or look up unknown words and references, as a reader does.

Many readers whose expectations have been shaped by screens expect a similar kind of spoon-feeding when reading books. They embrace stories that are easily digestible, with clearly labeled characters and little ambiguity. Perhaps this is why many adult readers now prefer the genre called young adult to any other. This rejection of the traditional responsibilities of the reader has resulted in a little-discussed deterioration of reading skills. Some writers respond by asking less and less of the reader, reducing the difficulty, complexity, and subtlety of their work. Together those writers and readers spiral into shallowness.

The reader who would redeem reading must cultivate a keen discernment, tasting and testing what is good and pursuing that. This, of course, is the responsibility of the Christian as well. Since readers and Christians are human and fallible, the main mass of either group tends to defer either to authority or to popular opinion, and to move in herds for safety. Herd animals are not known for their wisdom, however, nor for their reading acuity, and adopting the opinions of the herd will eventually lead any human being astray.[32] Each individual human being is responsible

---

32. Cf. Sarah Schulman, *The Gentrification of the Mind: Witness to a Lost Imagination* (Berkeley: University of California Press, 2012), 76: "The problem is that most people are average. This includes people who run universities, publishing companies, and the rewards system in the arts."

for tasting, testing, and deciding for himself whether a book falls into that small number that flow fresh and limpid as mountain streams, reviving and cleansing the mind, or whether it muddles, blears, and smudges the mind. As far as I can tell, no relationship exists between a book's success in the market and whether it belongs to the first category. Therefore, in addition to the ability to identify those books that deepen life, the reader must have the courage to trust his own taste and judgment, to love what he loves even if no one else agrees.

That reader's best instruments are careful, thoughtful questions. In terms of craft: How musical is the prose? How varied and effective are the sentence rhythms? Has the writer mastered language? Are words used precisely, applying their historical and etymological weight? One can tune one's ear for language most quickly by reading aloud metrical poetry across various eras, over and over, until syntax untangles and the sense of the poem is revealed. Compare the obsessive trochaic octameter of Poe's "The Raven" and Tennyson's "Locksley Hall" to Poe's cathedrals of prose sentences; Elizabeth Bishop's smooth lines to the cadenzas and glissandos of Woolf's; or the singsong simplicity of Marlowe's "The Passionate Shepherd to His Love" to Hemingway's constructions, and all of these to the flashing rapier work of Gerard Manley Hopkins' sonnets. One can observe the subtle operations of sound, rhythm, and the odd unexpected phrase upon an attentive listener. Painful but instructive contrasts can be found in Theo Marzials' "A Tragedy" or the verse of William McGonagall.

Diving into the poetry of all eras, one becomes aware that no human endeavor exists outside of history, and that all literature is an extended conversation. Reading poetry and other literature across centuries and countries makes a sculpture gallery of the mind, so that each solitary work appears in the context of the works that preceded it. As T. S. Eliot wrote, "No poet, no artist of any art, has his complete meaning alone. His significance, his appreciation is the appreciation of his relation to the dead poets and artists."[33] We do not fully understand a writer without knowing and grasping the work of her interlocutors, some of whom may be centuries gone, but to whom she is still responding. Authors are not inmates in solitary confinement, babbling to themselves, but singular voices joining a dialogue across the ages.

One must know and wrestle with Milton's Sonnet 19 to laugh a belly laugh at Ogden Nash's "Reminiscent Reflection," and one must have been enchanted by Marlowe's "The Passionate Shepherd" to smile at Dorothy Parker's "The Passionate Freudian to His Love," although the poems I pair here stand four hundred and five hundred years apart. Someone who notices that the lines "all your

33. T. S. Eliot, "Tradition and the Individual Talent," in *The Sacred Wood* (New York: Knopf, 1921), 44.

waves and your billows / passed over me" in Jonah 2:3 are a quotation from Psalm 42:7, or possibly the other way around, can recognize the consolatory power of poetry in the midst of affliction: how repeating the words of one who suffered in a prior century leaves neither alone in his suffering. The most powerful example is the opening of Psalm 22, which Christ cries out on the cross: "My God, my God, why have you forsaken me?" That Christ in his moment of greatest agony would quote a poet gives us an idea of what poets are here to do.

It is also useful to ask whether the author is trustworthy, not from suspicion but from pragmatism. We ought to ask the same about ourselves and others, in order to make sound and responsible decisions. In the context of reading, the question refers not to the author's personal life but to the quality of his work, because the encounter occurs in the work. For both nonfiction and fiction, the reader should consider the extent and solidity of the writer's research. Are citations from print or electronic sources? Are those sources independent, established, peer-reviewed, and fact-checked, or are they careless, biased, speculative, and dependent on shadowy funding? How good is the author's data? How accurately is information conveyed? If, in tracing a reference, I find the writer's assertions to be inaccurate or untrue, the data unreliable, or a compromised scientist presented as impartial expert, I know that I must verify other claims in that book.

Different modes of knowing have different uses and purposes, which I will sketch out lightly. Data, for example, is not the same thing as information, although the two are often confused. Data can be incompetently or maliciously collected and manipulated to tell convenient stories. If scrupulously collected and examined by those who know the difference between correlation and causation, between clinical endpoints and effects on mortality, and between longitudinal and cross-sectional studies, data can provide some amount of information, but this is not always the case.[34] Information only becomes knowledge when it is verified against reality, usually over the course of multiple trials. Knowledge, for example of the planets' orbits and relationships to the sun, tends to be revised over time, and so differs from truth, which exists and persists whether anyone is capable of grasping it.

Wisdom is less easy to describe. *Sapientia*, the Latin word for wisdom, derives from *sapio, sapere*, "to taste," which, like our other senses, can lead us to spit out what is harmful and ruminate upon what is good. We have defined our own species, *Homo sapiens*, by our ability to taste and to be wise, however rarely we live up to that aspiration. To be wise is to perceive the reality of a particular

---

34. As a crash course in the issues afflicting data collection and analysis and knowledge production, see *How to Lie with Statistics*, by Darrell Huff; *Data Pitfalls*, by Ben Jones; *How Charts Lie*, by Alberto Cairo; *How Not to Be Wrong*, by Jordan Ellenberg; and *The Misinformation Age*, by Cailin O'Connor and James Owen Weatherall.

situation or person at a given moment so completely and deeply that right action or speech, or right inaction or silence, reveals itself, and is chosen, an act continuous with and extending that understanding. Because wisdom is a living response to life, and life is chaotic and changes from moment to moment, wisdom cannot be reproduced through rules and rubrics. Two situations that appear identical may require entirely different actions just as two dishes can look the same, yet one be spoiled and the other delicious.

Finally there is revelation, as impossible to translate to others as a lightning strike, but no less powerful for that. Revelation produced Julian of Norwich's writings, and Jeanne Guyon's *Experiencing the Depths of Jesus Christ*,[35] and led Joan of Arc to command the French army at the age of seventeen. Whether one fears or desires it, revelation marks the full length of a life much as lightning marks a tree.

Mischief results when people mistake data for knowledge, knowledge for wisdom, and, more and more often, feelings for truth. One should not pilot a manned spacecraft by revelation, nor depend on data to explain what makes life worth living. But the present era is one of epistemological collapse. Processes and safeguards that once limited abuses of trust, including peer review at journals, fact-checking and relative neutrality at many newspapers,

---

35. Originally *A Short and Easy Method of Prayer.*

and the founding missions of respected institutions, have crumbled under the proliferation of academic publications, the pressure of diminishing budgets, and the weight of multimillion-dollar donations from billionaires pursuing their own agendas. Now more than ever, it is incumbent upon the reader, as it is upon every human being, to learn to distinguish between the various modes of knowing and the proper and improper uses of each. The task is exhausting, but abandoning it to others is to place oneself at the mercy of strangers, many of them motivated to fleece and deceive. It is the modern equivalent of bringing grain to a buyer without knowing weights, measures, and arithmetic.

Finally, the reader must have some sense of unspoken truth. Some ability to detect the desperation in a room full of convivial partygoers, the relief of a family after a protracted death, or the regret of a mother who never wanted her children is necessary for asking and answering the essential questions by which all literature is weighed. Does a novel awaken us to reality and the lovely, hideous, contradictory aspects of being human? Has the author observed human nature with love and wisdom, and does the author relate honestly what he has seen and learned? Or is the book nothing more than propaganda for one viewpoint or another, in which the characters are stamped out of sheet metal and machined to fit a political purpose?

The trouble with this requirement is that a reader can recognize falsity in a book only when that reader can recognize falsity in herself and in others, and truth in a book only when that reader has a sense of what is true. This means that the reader must collect enough firsthand knowledge of how human beings behave toward one another, in a mixture of circumstances, to notice when a writer has expressed a new insight about human nature, and when a writer is repeating popular platitudes. This sort of knowledge can only be acquired upon the skin-scraping rocks of reality, often through personal embroilment and at personal cost. Other people's experiences, filtered and mediated by books, films, television, theater, newspapers, and social media, will not suffice. These are the shadows dancing on the wall of Plato's cave, Peter London reminds us, and not reality itself.[36]

For related reasons, it is helpful to know at least one thing thoroughly, with all the senses, whether that is the flattening of a knife blank on an anvil, the shoeing of a horse, the piecing together of a garment or the coiling of a pot, the seasons of a forest, how to fight with fists or weapons, how to tend a hive, or how to read the weather, to give a few possibilities. This touchstone in material reality gives the reader a good chance of detecting shoddy work, cut corners, or imaginative fraud. Learning a craft or domain

---

36. London, *No More Secondhand Art*, 52.

of knowledge also teaches the reader respect for the honest efforts of others, as well as a sense of the different magnitudes of toil and skill between creating what is good and what is excellent.

The Christian likewise must spend time in the presence of Christ, arguing, pleading, or sitting quietly and listening, for hours and days and years on end, learning the sound of His voice and the color and breadth and depth of His being, to avoid being misled by impersonations or false claims to His authority. A scam email purporting to be from a distant acquaintance will fool us more easily than one from someone we speak to every day. Similarly, we should be able to recognize when a sermon says what He never would.

Even after acquiring these skills, the reader must also give a kind of consent to the work, "without which," Jacques Maritain writes, "we cannot be taken into the confidence of the poem." If we grant that consent, however, if we allow the work to operate upon us, we receive in return the poet's "transient and incomparable knowing."[37] Not every work deserves this degree of trust, for which reason I have listed the skills and questions that allow anyone to thresh and winnow the grain from the chaff. But if we close our hearts to that which has the power to transfigure,

---

37. Jacques Maritain, *Creative Intuition in Art and Poetry* (Providence, RI: Cluny Media, 2018), 282–283.

which must always be startlingly new,[38] then however extensive our knowledge and experience, and however magnificent the book, it will have little effect upon us. We will miss its gift entirely. God loves us but does not force His love upon those unwilling to receive it, and the same is true of lesser authors who nevertheless have craft, skill, and love to offer.

To read in the way I have suggested here is nothing more and nothing less than to live with open eyes and ears, attuned to both the sharp edge of the present and the thick layers of the past. It is to see not what we wish to see, or what other people tell us that we see, but what is really in front of us. It is to fully inhabit our bodies and our lives, in order to recognize what is vibrant, vital, and life-giving, whether in people, places, or books. It is to thoroughly learn, as a lover studies the beloved, the language we read in, that we may recognize landmarks and birthmarks, what is nourishing and what is diseased. The same, of course, is required of writers, who are and must be readers first.

---

38. See Marcel Proust, *Within a Budding Grove*, vol. 1, trans. C. K. Scott Moncrieff (New York: Thomas Seltzer, 1924), 327: "A well-read man will at once begin to yawn with boredom when anyone speaks to him of a new 'good book,' because he imagines a sort of composite of all the good books that he has read and knows already, whereas a good book is something special, something incalculable, and is made up not of the sum of all previous masterpieces but of something which the most thorough assimilation of every one of them would not enable him to discover, since it exists not in their sum but beyond it." Found in Elaine Scarry's *On Beauty and Being Just* (Princeton, NJ: Princeton University Press, 1999).

No collaboration and no real partnership are possible when one partner remains passive or declines to learn and grow. This is as true of the act of reading, which is properly a collaboration between reader and writer, as it is of our relationship with God. Only when readers have the skills of discernment, close reading, scansion, careful weighing of evidence and argument, good judgment, and openness to what is worthy though unfamiliar can they demand the literature that requires these skills. Only when a sufficient number of skillful readers exist does a writer have a chance of publishing such a work, and another after that. Otherwise, they flower briefly and die in the dark.

⌒

The Puritan conflation of reading with the production of virtue is not limited to literature. Some well-intentioned Christians make similarly inflated claims about reading the Bible. They may insist that others read the Bible daily, or on a military schedule, like taking doses of castor oil. It is true that a basic knowledge of the Bible has always been beneficial to Christians as well as to students of literature, and that Scripture can teach, admonish, encourage, and console. It is easy to forget the sacrifices of those who sought to make the Bible more widely available, from William Tyndale, who was convicted of heresy, strangled, and burned for translating the Bible into English and distributing it, to Li Guangqiang, who was imprisoned for smuggling Chinese-language Bibles into China. At the same time, we should remember that Satan quotes Scripture for his own ends, and be careful to ask in prayer what and how and when we should read.

It is possible to replace God with the Bible, and to worship the letter of the text in ignorance and cruelty. Moreover, Ghiberti's Gates of Paradise, Byzantine mosaics, and stained-glass windows and frescos in churches from Europe to Africa to Asia bear mute witness to those generations who lived in faith without direct access to the Bible, other than what could be gleaned from sermons, stories, and art. I do not think that those who loved and obeyed God in those days had faith any smaller than those who love and obey God now.

A colleague once told me that although she prayed often and had a close relationship with God, she had been raised in a literalist church that she later left, and now did not read the Bible, because she was not sure that she believed in it. She felt guilty about her failure to read. When it came to my own friends, I told her, I most cherished the time I spent with them, whether we were fishing, hiking, or telling each other what was on our minds and hearts. It did not matter to me whether they read my books or not, though I was grateful if they did. A few understood me better for having done so, but at least one person made incorrect assumptions about me as a result. If I, being small and vain, do not fret over whether my friends read what I write, how much deeper and richer is the heart of God?

In the same way that I am not trying to discourage the reading of other books, I do not discourage reading the Bible. But I would warn Christians against putting anything, including the Bible, above God, as Pharisees past and present put the Law above Christ.[39]

I first read the Bible most of the way through when I was eight years old, on a trip to visit family in rural China, because apart from a collection of historical jokes picked up at a bookstore in Beijing, the Bible I had been made to pack was the only English-language material to be found for hundreds of miles. When I was not collecting eggs from straw-lined baskets, chasing grasshoppers that rose in a hissing wave, catching frogs, or shelling beans, I waxed wroth over Jephthah's daughter, Elijah's bears, and God's decisions more generally. I skipped the endless begats. Very little made sense to me at the time.

It would take two decades for me to learn that the richest approach to the Bible is not linear and all at once, but

---

39. "Sad, indeed, would the whole matter be, if the Bible had told us *everything* God meant us to believe. But herein is the Bible itself greatly wronged. It nowhere lays claim to be regarded as *the* Word, *the* Way, *the* Truth. The Bible leads us to Jesus, the inexhaustible, the ever unfolding Revelation of God. It is Christ 'in whom are hid all the treasures of wisdom and knowledge,' not the Bible, save as leading to Him." George MacDonald, "The Higher Faith," in *Unspoken Sermons: First Series* (New York: Longmans, Green, and Co., 1906), 52–53.

fragment by fragment, and not by reading with the eyes but living it out with every atom of my being. I found that I could not choose which passages my days would be grated through like horseradish, nor at what time. I would not have picked two rounds of Job, if anyone had bothered to ask, nor a lonely stint as Noah's raven. Neither did I particularly enjoy Joseph's years of waiting and praying in prison, asking God in confusion what the dreams were for, whether God was still there, or whether those dreams had been delusion.

But though Genesis is silent on this point, I now know something of Joseph's pleas and complaints to God in the decade that he was unjustly imprisoned.[40] I can say with confidence, as no scholar can or should, that in addition to waiting on God with patience and endurance, Joseph must have raged, wept, and doubted, because he was a human being, as am I. Anyone who has been assigned those chapters to live through is likely to reach the same understanding.

While shut up in prison, Joseph also must have praised God. Watchman Nee, who spent the final twenty years of his life imprisoned for his faith, observes that even those who do not believe in God sometimes say "Thank God" and "Hallelujah" when good things happen. But only those who love God are able, in darkness and distress, to praise and thank God through our tears, and thereby offer up the "sacrifice of praise" described in Hebrews 13:15. In

---

40. One of the advantages I had over the biblical Joseph was Wayne Stiles' excellent *Waiting on God* (Grand Rapids, MI: BakerBooks, 2015).

that moment, we proclaim God's victory. As with Peter and Silas, who praised God and sang hymns in prison, our chains fall off, and we are free.[41] Nee himself had been influenced by the work of Jeanne Guyon, who was falsely accused and imprisoned for years at a time in the Convent of St. Marie, the Bastille, and Vincennes, and yet who wrote, perhaps during one of those periods, a hymn of purest freedom, which includes the lines: "But prison walls cannot control / The flight, the freedom of the soul."

My understanding of 1 Kings 13, the story of the man of God and the lion, also changed over time. The "man of God," as he is described, walked from Judah to Bethel to stand before a king and prophesy against him, at great risk to his own life, in obedience to God. Having received an order from God to "neither eat bread nor drink water nor return by the way that you came," he declines the king's offer of a meal and a gift and takes another road, but is tricked by an old prophet into sitting down for dinner. He is killed by a lion as the result of his disobedience. Like so much in the Bible, the story struck me as brutally unfair. Death by lion seemed like a disproportionate punishment for eating dinner.

But over the years, because I have occasionally listened to the still, small voice that tells me to rise up and go, even if nothing in a particular situation strikes me as wrong,

---

41. Watchman Nee, *Praising* (Anaheim, CA: Living Stream Ministry, 1993), 4, 8.

and at other times I have ignored it, to my subsequent regret, I began to suspect that I misunderstood that chapter. 1 Peter 5:8 reminds us that "the devil prowls around like a roaring lion, seeking someone to devour." I now think that God knew of the lion and its path, and that He was hurrying His beloved servant home ahead of it. I have also learned that the courage to defy kings at God's command does not spring up overnight but grows from years of slow, small steps taken in faith. I do not think God would have willingly lost or willfully disposed of such a person when they are so rare to begin with and take so long to develop.

I cannot prove my claim. Those who have struggled with that passage, who now hear it vibrate with a sweet, pure note, need no more than that. I give it as an illustration of the confounding and unintuitive order of reading, then living, then grasping a passage of the Bible. The fruit of the tree of knowledge is not the fruit of the tree of life.[42] In sermon after sermon, novel after novel, MacDonald reminds us that we cannot know the living God without listening to and then obeying Him. Understanding is only given after obedience.[43] The understanding he

---

42. L'Engle has suggested that God may have intended to offer the fruits of the first tree at the proper time, when human beings had sufficiently matured in their life with God. Madeleine L'Engle, *The Rock That Is Higher: Story as Truth* (Wheaton, IL: Harold Shaw Publishers, 1993), 205–206.

43. One example from MacDonald's *The Hope of the Gospel* (London: Ward, Lock, Bowden, and Co., 1892), 17–19: "Men would understand: they do not

describes is not academic in nature. It is not discovered at seminary but after living and wrestling with God, and it is not given to us when we demand it but when God wills. In this, MacDonald echoes Julian of Norwich, who wrote five hundred years earlier that all anyone can do is "seke [God], suffer, and trust.... And the clernesse of finding, it is of his special grace when it is his will."[44]

One comes to a real understanding of the Bible, or of God, only when the time is ripe, and only after giving a more profound consent than the reader of poetry gives the poem. By this I mean the willingness to read the text with one's whole life. Only by reading at this depth do we receive whatever instruction, revelation, or transformation has been prepared for us.

This too is a partnership. As every writer knows, even the highest, most monumental work of literature will not be consummated, and bears no fruit, without at least one reader who is willing to bring to the text her whole heart

---

care to *obey*,—understand where it is impossible they should understand save by obeying. They would search into the work of the Lord instead of doing their part in it—thus making it impossible both for the Lord to go on with his work, and for themselves to become capable of seeing and understanding what he does....By obedience, I intend no kind of obedience to man, or submission to authority claimed by man or community of men. I mean obedience to the will of the Father, however revealed in our conscience...Upon obedience our energy must be spent; understanding will follow."

44. Second Revelation, Chapter 10, in *The Writings of Julian of Norwich*, edited by Nicholas Watson and Jacqueline Jenkins (University Park, PA: Penn State University Press, 2006), 161.

and her whole soul and her whole mind. Neither will creation be completed until it is read, the way a mother reads a story to her child. Our task is to read and to listen, and also, perhaps, to interject and question and argue at times. Once in a while we may even persuade the Storyteller to change the course of the story, because of His love and delight in us. And once the reading is finished, and the book of the world rolled up like a scroll, who knows but that the next story will not be a better one?

II

Chapter Three

VOCATION

Most popular guides to writing a book suggest that anyone can do it and that everyone should. They may offer a special method or formula, and they may enumerate the benefits that accrue to the writer, in a list as long as those attributed to Victorian nostrums or Venetian theriaca: money, fame, love, psychological healing, influence, self-esteem, status, family and societal approval. While people have written for all of these reasons for as long as books have existed, and sometimes have achieved their aims, to write a book with a focus on what the writer will get from readers, rather than what the writer gives, is a mistake. Like nostrums or theriaca, which variously contained mercury, lead, opium, and powdered vipers, the book that results will at best do no harm and at worst sicken the recipient.

Comparatively few people speak about what it means to write, or more precisely, to be written through, in the service of God, or Truth, or Art.[1] The most useful remarks I have found come from George MacDonald, G. K. Chesterton, Jacques and Raïssa Maritain, James Baldwin, Madeleine L'Engle, Annie Dillard, Czesław Miłosz, and Christian Wiman. As far as I am concerned, to write or create for these higher purposes, for life and life's flourishing, the artist must draw from the deep wells in her being water for the river of eternity, for the use of past and future generations, rather than seeking to please and often compromising herself for a fickle readership in the present. Both artists and Christians serve God by completing the tasks that are given to them, whatever they may be. The result may be a book, or a fence, or a meal; the work may be writing, or rolling wine barrels, as Brother Lawrence did, or speaking soft words into strife. But in each of these cases the service, the achievement, and the Master are the same.

We are responsible for doing the work set before us to the best of our ability. The world's reception of the work is not our concern.

---

1. For me these are all names for the same One.

Any book usually takes the writer several years to write, and the reader hours to read. In this sense it represents an irrevocable exchange of life far beyond whatever price the reader pays at the register and the one or two dollars the writer receives as a result. In literature, the implicit promise is that the writer has taken pains to make a book worthy of the time the reader spends reading it. Annie Dillard puts the matter starkly: "Write as if you were dying. At the same time, assume you write for an audience consisting of terminal patients. That is, after all the case."[2]

The writer who would follow that injunction must have, or else acquire, integrity, honesty, a fine and discerning judgment in choosing subjects and stories, skill in the craft, care for language, and respect for the reader's life and intelligence.[3] To write conscious of the mayfly lives of both writer and reader, here for a flash and gone, means reaching for what is real, meaningful, and conducive to growth over what is spurious, frivolous, and degrading, and to say what must be said as concisely as possible, without wasting words. While developing one's craft, one can write whatever and however one likes, but when writing for publication, I do my best to follow Dillard's ethic.

---

2. Annie Dillard, *The Writing Life* (New York: HarperPerennial, 2013), 68.
3. By *respect* I mean a loving regard for another living human being with only so many days on this earth, which can include disagreement and healthy challenges to think and grow. I do not mean deference, agreement, reassurance, fear, or flattery.

The writer who writes a book that nourishes and gives life, the kind of book that is like bread, satisfying hunger, as Miłosz said of true poems, reenacts the meal where Love once blessed and broke five loaves and two fishes and fed the multitude. To do otherwise is to leave the seeking thousands hungry. Christian Wiman observes that "Art, like religious devotion, either adds life or steals it. It is never neutral."[4] Within any book or other work of art there is an indefinable space wherein we find that gift of life, or else a vacuity and a lack. The presence or absence of that gift can be recognized by the subjective experience it produces in the sensitive and attentive reader. That is to say, a book may function as a blood transfusion or as a vampire's bite. It may remind us of the joy, absurdity, and tragedy that are the inheritance of every human being, of the blessing that is air to breathe, the pleasure of clean water to drink, and the bliss of clover under bare feet. Or it may swallow our hours without reciprocation, leave us drained and diminished, and teach us contempt toward other people, the book, and the reader's self.

Many books, of course, fall between these extremes. Some only offer their gift at a certain phase of the reader's life, and not after or before. Whether a book gives life or takes it is independent of the book's genre, topic, and tone,

---

4. Christian Wiman, *My Bright Abyss: Meditation of a Modern Believer* (New York: Farrar, Straus and Giroux, 2013), 100.

Wiman notes.[5] It is a quality that is impossible to prove to others and private to each reader's experience. Yet I have met readers who share my sense of it, who directed me to other books possessing this quality, which to me is more important than genre, topic, or tone.

I have sketched here the reader's perspective of this quality, this gift that I call love and believe necessary to creation, to provide an idea of what the true artist is aiming at. For the writer who would create in this way, giving life and honoring it, it is crucial to work from the correct source and with the proper orientation.

By correct *source*, I refer to Erich Fromm's conception of love as giving of what is alive in oneself, and to Czesław Miłosz's definition of poetry as "the passionate pursuit of the Real."[6] The skillful writer who writes from his own aliveness, from his own encounters with reality, will produce writing that is fresh and vivid, that rings the reader's being like a bell. The effect is intensified if the writer is also writing out of the One who is Life and Truth. To write from such sources, the writer need not be happy or optimistic. The writer does require, however, an undistorted firsthand experience of life in all its aspects, including experience of that Life that is greater.

---

5. Wiman, *My Bright Abyss*, 100.
6. Czesław Miłosz, *The Witness of Poetry* (Cambridge, MA: Harvard University Press, 1983), 56.

By correct *orientation*, I mean that when the artist is creating, and when the Christian is doing his works in the world, both ought to be giving rather than taking, whether that is giving light, speaking life, or sharing carefully and precisely the angle of sunlight that fell across the glasses and glazed mugs of a table set for breakfast. One's attention, speech, and art are directed outward, toward others. For women in particular, I would emphasize that this does not mean *niceness*, which is often oriented inward. It does not mean permitting abuse, parasitic behavior, entitled demands, or emotional manipulation; indiscriminate giving; submitting to other people's thefts of property, dignity, or time; or disclosing private information when pressed to do so. It is a wise and measured giving, at the Spirit's leading, firmly bounded and when appropriate. It can mean administering discipline to others for the sake of their maturity and the growth of the church, or giving someone the space and opportunity to make mistakes and learn from them.

Differences in orientation often become visible after reading many books or watching many presentations. One speaker will pour out her knowledge and experience to anyone who listens, while another absorbs the attention of the audience, directing her focus and answers inward, and speaks for her personal gratification. One book charms, tap-dances, and performs sleight-of-hand tricks to delight the reader, while another, written to indulge the author's vanity, appears as tightly involuted as those double-bloom dahlias that, while pretty, offer no footing or food to bees.

I am not interested in making proper orientation a moral stricture. The outward-flowing orientation that I describe cannot be permanent, because human beings must also receive, retreat, and recover, especially in times of sickness, weakness, or need, or else be utterly exhausted. Moreover, technical, theoretical, and emotional problems can be worked out on private pages without attending to source and orientation. But when we are creating what we mean to become public, we ought to seek the proper orientation and the deepest, truest source, however short we fall of these things, or we have no chance at producing incandescent work.

Few writers think or work in this way at present. Those who write in this way have at different times described those who do not, and those accounts, taken together, provide a useful taxonomy. Dillard's false artists are the self-absorbed youths who dislike reading but wish to be admired as writers, as well as those who write books with movie options in mind.[7] Wiman's are those who write for others' approval, for self-promotion, and for self-perpetuation.[8] Jacques Maritain's false and failed artists include those who, in rushing to show off, fail to listen for the leading of life, or Life, which he calls poetic

7. Dillard, *The Writing Life*, 18, 70.
8. Wiman, *My Bright Abyss*, 45.

intuition; those who write "for the psychotherapeutic release of the repressed dreams and sex obsessions of his tormented reader"; and those who confuse art and partisanship.[9] I myself would add those who write out of a hermetic and impenetrable self-interest, who have self-justification, the gratification of base desires and drives, or the calculated manipulation of others as their aim.

These counterfeit artists, Maritain says, have all substituted ego for the higher, intuitive "creative Self," resulting in "so many works which have nothing or little to say."[10] Or, as Paul said: "If I speak in the tongues of men and of angels, but have not love, I am a noisy gong or a clanging cymbal" (1 Cor. 13:1). My point here is that, in order to create a work that can sustain the human spirit, the artist's creativity must be directed outward, and the artist must begin in love and create out of that. To make a work that endures, the artist must also listen to, and disappear into, that which is higher and greater than him, and eternal.

For the writers I have cited above, and in my own experience, true creation involves the submission of the skilled and practiced human being to whatever sliver of Life or Art or Love seeks to move through him into the world.[11]

---

9. Jacques Maritain, *Creative Intuition in Art and Poetry* (Providence, RI: Cluny Media, 2018), 125, 178.

10. Maritain, *Creative Intuition in Art and Poetry*, 125.

11. Cf. Martin Buber, *I and Thou*, trans. Walter Kaufmann (New York: Simon and Schuster, 1970), 60. Buber says that all art begins when "a human

A transformative artwork is not and has never been about the artist through whom it comes into being. While the original conception may be perfect in potentia, its birth is a protracted, perilous labor. What emerges is partial and imperfect until and unless the artist willingly dies to self and becomes a hollow pipe through which the art flows. "Channels only, blessed Master," goes the hymn, and this is the artist's prayer as well. We pray to be scoured of every trace of the egoic self, of blockages and obstacles, resentment and guilt, so that power, blessing, and life may stream freely through us and out of us. Should we succeed, we become so many brushes in the Artist's hand, useful and used.

This is not a new revelation. "The progress of an artist is a continual self-sacrifice, a continual extinction of personality," T. S. Eliot wrote in 1919. "What happens is a continual surrender of himself as he is at the moment to something which is more valuable."[12] The process Eliot describes is perhaps most perfectly illustrated by Annie Dillard's observation, in *Holy the Firm*, of a moth that flew

---

being confronts a form that wants to become a work through him." It is "imperious"; it "demands the soul's creative power"; it requires "a deed that a man does with his whole being: if he commits it and speaks with his being the basic word to the form that appears, then the creative power is released and the work comes into being." While I read Buber only after turning in the revised draft of this book, I have come to many of the same conclusions.
12. T. S. Eliot, "Tradition and the Individual Talent," in *The Sacred Wood* (New York: Knopf, 1921), 47. The order of the two sentences is reversed.

near a candle flame, became caught in the soft wax, and burned as a second wick for hours, with liquid wax drawn up through its hollowed body.[13] This is the artist's vocation, and the Christian's. We are created with a body of dust and, once pupated, an unutterable longing for light, even though the fate of our kind is to search, reproduce, and die in the dark. But Dillard's moth brushed against the light that called to it, and for hours the moth was a conduit for that same light, doubling it, shining out into the darkness where the other moths flew.

Poe describes this yearning with the same metaphor in "The Poetic Principle":

> We still have a thirst unquenchable....It is the desire of the moth for the star. It is no mere appreciation of the Beauty before us—but a wild effort to reach the Beauty above....We weep then—not as the Abbaté Gravina supposes—through excess of pleasure, but through a certain, petulant, impatient sorrow at our inability to grasp *now*, wholly, here on earth, at once and forever, those divine and rapturous joys, of which *through* the poem, or *through* the music, we attain to but brief and indeterminate glimpses.[14]

---

13. Annie Dillard, *Holy the Firm* (New York: HarperCollins, 2007), 15–16.
14. Edgar Allan Poe, "The Poetic Principle," in *The Works of Edgar Allan Poe*, vol. 1 (New York: Funk and Wagnalls, 1904), 30–31.

The high purpose of the artist is to open, through her art, so many windows to the stars, providing those brief glimpses of the light of eternity, that "Beauty above," that gives such joy and grief. The writer in particular searches for truth, listening and digging and toiling for it, and for the exact and perfect verbalization of the truth.

When the artist's source is God, the artist becomes a prophet in the oldest sense of the word, saying what God has given her to say. Like the prophet, the artist must learn to listen for that still small voice in the depths of her being, for that faint sense of a task being set before her. Prayer and meditation are helpful in this regard. It is for this reason that L'Engle says that "the disciplines of the creative process and Christian contemplation are almost identical."[15] While this attitude and practice of listening does not appear in arts or creative writing curricula, it is indispensable to the artistic process.

Be it God or Art who passes through the writer, as a royal personage might deign to pass through one's house and into the garden, a certain amount of preparation is called for. One tidies and airs out the soul's domicile, chops down the thorn hedge of the ego, and wipes the windows, so that nothing disturbs or interrupts the procession. The significance of the occasion lies neither in the house nor in the owner, who lingers invisibly to adjust the

---

15. Madeleine L'Engle, *Walking on Water* (New York: North Point Press, 2000), 185.

curtains, but in the Person or power, call it what you will, who is transiting through that house.[16]

What I am getting at is a rare and requisite degree of transparency in the artist. Without this, no real art is possible. It is the transparency of the glass chimney of an oil lamp, which guards and reveals the kerosene flame within. The glass chimney is not responsible for shining into the darkness, because the glass is not the source of the light, but it can either faithfully transmit that shining or else dim and hinder it. It is the artist's duty to keep the glass clean of dust and soot. The greater the transparency, which is to say, the less one sees of the glass, the brighter the light can burn.

This brings us to the twenty-first century's primary misunderstanding about writing and art. Writing is not self-expression but the death of the self.[17] To create any art that affirms life, L'Engle notes, "the artist must die."[18] Eliot writes that genuine poetry is not the expression of personality or emotion, but an escape from those things.[19]

Self-expression is opacity. It interposes a monolithic ego, along with the heaped stones of personal grievances and opinions, between the innermost light and the world.

---

16. One must of course have a house to begin with, that is, a fully developed soul, in order to offer it up. Along the same lines, one's old self can hardly be crucified (Rom. 6:6) if it hasn't been formed in the first place.

17. A temporary death; like a thorn hedge, ego regrows.

18. L'Engle, *Walking on Water*, 193.

19. T. S. Eliot, "Tradition and the Individual Talent," 52–53.

However bright the flame, very little of its glow can pass such a barrier. Only gleams will escape, here and there, if at all. Virginia Woolf, glancing over *Jane Eyre*, says of Charlotte Brontë, "She will never get her genius expressed whole and entire.... She will write of herself where she should write of her characters."[20] For Eliot, again, the bad poet is "unconscious where he ought to be conscious, and conscious where he ought to be unconscious," and the result is that he becomes too "personal" in his poem.[21] There is nothing objectionable about self-expression in and of itself. It can be a private enjoyment, a relief from misery, or the first motions of a new-molted personality. The young artist begins there, though it is a pity if she does not advance. But there is also nothing high or holy about self-expression. Relentlessly pursued by the artist, it obstructs the creation of art.

Various bodily emissions, like blood and mucus, can be described with painful literalism as self-expressions. A sneeze is a self-expression. It is natural to sneeze, but one hopes not to do so while performing a flute concerto. Parents are honor-bound to stick their child's crayoned scrawls to the refrigerator and to handle that child's effluvia for several years. After that, it is no longer reasonable for the child to share every scrawl and every sneeze, much

---

20. Virginia Woolf, *A Room of One's Own* (San Diego: Harcourt, 1989), 69–70.
21. Eliot, "Tradition and the Individual Talent," 52.

less demand universal praise for them. The acquisition of any degree of taste, and the initial development of artistic judgment, is usually sufficient to keep the practice work hidden, out of healthy embarrassment, and the chrysalid phrase private, as it is meant to be.

⌒

The artist dies to self, burns, and becomes transparent not out of self-hatred but out of love, so that something greater than the self might come into being. It is a hollowing and a hallowing. To be an artist, Baldwin says, requires "a willingness to give up everything…you and who you think you are, who you think you'd like to be, where you'd think you'd like to go—everything, and this forever, forever."[22] Mary Oliver reminds us that "creative work requires a loyalty as complete as the loyalty of water to the force of gravity…. He who does not crave that roofless place *eternity* should stay at home."[23] Jesus said in invitation and warning, "If anyone would come after me, let him deny himself and take up his cross and follow me" (Matt. 16:24). Much as I wish it were otherwise, again and again I discover the truth of these words. At a moment's notice, one has to set aside what the world thinks valuable,

22. Baldwin, "The Artist's Struggle for Integrity," in *The Cross of Redemption*, 55.
23. Mary Oliver, "Of Power and Time," in *Blue Pastures* (New York: Harcourt, 1995), 6.

what *I* had thought valuable, whether that is a home, a job, friendships, a church community, one's good name, or financial stability, for the sake of what is higher. Christian or not, the true artist walks by faith and not by sight, each of us like Abraham, who "when called to go to a place he would later receive as his inheritance, obeyed and went, even though he did not know where he was going" (Heb. 11:8 NIV). When we are called in this way, we obey and go, even though we cannot see what lies ahead. One steps into, and becomes, something altogether new.

Although I describe the death of the artist's self, it is not physical death that is demanded of us, which comes to everyone in its own time, but living: a whole life, subjected to study, practice, failure, encounter, and discipline. We can grant or withhold our consent to be transfigured by such a living, as a reader can assent to, or refuse, a transformative book. We are not spared the formative events, however. As the blacksmith heats steel to the color of butter and beats it into a form fit for use, repeatedly returning the metal to the furnace, so we are burnt, beaten, and shaped by incidents and catastrophes in our lives, which, if we are willing, if we bend with the blows, make us more of what we must be. "Break, blow, burn, and make me new," is Donne's immortal prayer. He had made himself one thing before learning God's intended form for him, and bent to the remaking, though in the end neither shape of him was wasted.

Forging generally strengthens steel, aligning the grain of the metal and driving out inclusions. Self-pity interrupts the process. Complaining to God, arguing with God, and vociferously remonstrating with God in the midst of suffering, however, are perfectly acceptable, and number among the favorite pastimes of the prophets in the Bible.[24] The prophets had plenty of reasons to complain. Always the artist, or writer, or prophet is worked upon, or more bluntly, worked over, as a knife is first forged then ground to sharpness, so that it can cut and carve and create. It is very unpleasant. I know of no exceptions.

The metal billet experiences the furnace, the hammer, and the metal grinder without knowing the reason for these things. The suffering is, to all appearances, sense-less. When I was about eleven years old, I was forbidden to read fiction, because fiction was lies, and therefore satanic. Going forward, I was told, my hoarded novels would be thrown away, and I would only be permitted nonfiction and the Bible.[25] I thought the prohibition stupid and unjust. With every particle of my being, I resisted it. When the hammer blows ceased, and the fiery heat was quenched, I was toughened. I would never again permit my parents or any church authority to be the arbiters of my life and decisions. From that point on, no human being would have the power to discourage me from

24. See most of Psalms, the Book of Job, and all of Lamentations.
25. I have purposefully understated the matter.

writing, or to pass judgment on my soul. Though I did not know it then, that was the first real step I took toward meeting and knowing God.[26]

Those people in the world, strangers and near-strangers, who believe they have the ability to hurt me with their words, do not know how many armies were massed against me when I was a child—at eleven, at fourteen, at sixteen. I survived them. The experience may be a common one for those whom God calls to become artists, although I did not know it then. One seldom realizes, within that all-consuming darkness, that one is not alone. More than a decade later, three things happened in a single year: I heard an acclaimed actress, a firm Christian, describe praying to God as a child that He let her die, as I had done; I read bell hooks' *All About Love*, describing her own longing to die in her youth, and the divine love that stopped her;[27] and I was able to tell a young artist, still walking in that valley's shadow, that she was not alone, and that the darkness would not remain forever.

I do not think it a coincidence that the three of us who have developed into mature artists all acknowledge a loving God who had plans for us, who called us onward to

---

26. I suspect that anyone who has not accepted full responsibility for his own life, who cedes it to others and blindly believes what they tell him God wants, cannot know God as a living Person. He can only do so when he steps into his own life and looks for himself.

27. bell hooks, *All About Love: New Visions* (New York: William Morrow, 2001), 225, 235.

light and life, nor that we all suffered a similar pattern of attack. What greater threat to the rulers and authorities and powers of darkness than a moth that, for the love of light, is willing to join itself to flame? How many more might learn to do the same? Darkness would be driven back before that extravagant love. It would be better, for those who rule only where darkness falls, to crush that moth before it catches fire. While it is difficult to destroy a grown artist at the height of her powers, a child is exquisitely vulnerable. I would not be surprised to learn that many did not survive.

In adulthood, the artist undergoes a lengthy process of sanctification, which is a pretty word for an unpleasant experience. To sanctify something is to make it holy and wholly dedicated to God. That which becomes holy, be it lamb, ox, craft, firstfruits, or dream, is offered up to God, becoming His. He may consume our offering with fire and give us holy ashes in the place of cherished hopes, or He may return what we gave Him, beautifully transformed. The paradox here is that, once trained and mature, the artist must be willing to offer up artmaking itself, must be willing to walk away from art, in order to be perfected as an artist. Until that moment, when Aquinas fell silent, strong marks of the self remain. One clings to one's status, one's skill, one's identity as an artist, as others cling to job titles, political affiliations, and family roles, to avoid standing a naked human being in the vastness of eternity, seeing that we are like grass that withers, and finding, in that moment, that we are staggeringly loved.

One winter I prayed, as someone suggested, "Lord, if You love me, show me. Prove it." What followed was a fire that consumed everything I trusted and counted on. The job I delighted in became a nightmare, and after seven tortuous months, I was asked to resign. My heart began to stutter and skip beats, until I saw a surgeon who burned a small portion away. I was forced to walk by faith. At every turn, what I needed was somehow provided, even when I did not know I needed it. Mercies piled upon mercies. I resigned myself to the knowledge that I was loved. A little more than a year after I prayed that reckless prayer, I offered up what I had withheld for over a decade, since the time I had been told that fiction was evil, when I decided I would never surrender it. Responding to His abundant proofs of love, I said: God, if you want me to give up on the novel and the years of work, if this is not Your will, if you want me to stop writing — I will.

The answer came suddenly, warm as spring: I am the *Author*...[28]

I laughed.

Finish the book, I was told.

Two hard years would pass, full of doubt and rejections and forced stillness, before the promise was fulfilled, and

---

28. See Hebrews 12:2 KJV.

the book published, but that time was of less importance than the revisions He had been making in me.

Suffering and loss are inescapable, no matter what one chooses to do, or how one lives. But although I have enumerated the costs of this particular vocation, the rewards far exceed them. A hammer in the hand of a carpenter is fulfilling the purpose for which it was made. Through it, houses, beehives, and dinner tables come into the world. It strikes each blow with satisfaction. An artist, put to the use for which he is made, experiences the same deep satisfaction and fulfillment. There is also pure joy in reaching, after prolonged exertion, a creative breakthrough. Rollo May suggests that in such moments we are experiencing an echo of God's joy in His creation, of things being as they are meant to be.[29] However briefly, we participate in the divine intention for the world. It is a foretaste of the kingdom of God.[30] Both artist and Christian are invited to enter into this joy.

There is a more glorious promise than this. Paul writes, in 1 Corinthians 15:58, "Always give yourselves fully to the work of the Lord, because you know that your labor in the Lord is not in vain" (NIV). N. T. Wright interprets that verse in this way: "Every act of love, gratitude, and kindness; every work of art or music inspired by the love of

---

29. Rollo May, *The Courage to Create* (New York: W. W. Norton, 1975), 122.
30. See Madeleine L'Engle, *The Rock That Is Higher* (Wheaton, IL: Harold Shaw Publishers, 1993), 22.

God and delight in the beauty of his creation...will find its way, through the resurrecting power of God, into the new creation."[31] That is, something of what we make or do today, as artists or Christians led by God, will outlive not only us but the present creation, and be added to the new. Makoto Fujimura, commenting on Wright, finds a more explicit statement of that hope in 1 Corinthians 3:12–14: "Now if anyone builds on the foundation with gold, silver, precious stones, wood, hay, straw—each one's work will become manifest, for the Day will disclose it, because it will be revealed by fire, and the fire will test what sort of work each one has done. If the work that anyone has built on the foundation survives, he will receive a reward." This passage is usually understood as a warning, but Fujimura points out that it contains an extraordinary promise: that what sound and lasting work we do on the foundation of Christ will pass through the purifying fire and be revealed as beautiful and indestructible at the end of days.[32] How carefully, how joyfully would we work if we held this hope and beheld this promise, that everything done well, with divine love as its source, will not only survive this world but contribute to the next?

---

31. N. T. Wright, *Surprised by Hope: Rethinking Heaven, the Resurrection, and the Mission of the Church* (New York: HarperOne, 2008), 208.
32. Makoto Fujimura, *Art and Faith* (New Haven, CT: Yale University Press, 2021), 128. I am indebted to Fujimura's book for the pointer to N. T. Wright's.

Every person, I believe, has been created with a holy and royal purpose. Each one of us has been placed on this planet to do at least one beautiful thing that no one else is capable of doing, as long as we assent to that purpose and the preparation, discipline, and long working out of it. For Jerome Hines, that purpose included singing in the role of Boris Godunov before Nikita Khrushchev in Moscow during the Cuban Missile Crisis, and singing in many Salvation Army and YMCA meetings before that.[33] For George MacDonald, that purpose included preaching true, beautiful, and unorthodox sermons to a congregation that rejected him, sermons that were nevertheless read by many others over centuries; writing the novel that turned C. S. Lewis from atheism to Christianity; and penning fairy tales that delighted Mark Twain's children as well as, much later, Jane Yolen.[34]

---

33. In *A Stone for a Pillow* (New York: Convergent, 2017), 94, L'Engle suggests that Hines prevented the outbreak of nuclear war with his reinterpretation of the opera's final scene, Boris Godunov's abdication, as glorious rather than humiliating, along with his blessing of Khrushchev at the post-performance reception. Hines himself is much more modest about his accomplishment. He says simply that he was the first American to realize there would be no war, based on Khrushchev's words and attitude at that reception. Jerome Hines, *This Is My Story, This Is My Song* (Westwood, NJ: Fleming H. Revell Company, 1968), 138–158.
34. Yolen describes loving and teaching and rereading *The Golden Key* over forty years in her afterword to *The Golden Key*, by George MacDonald (Grand Rapids, MI: Eerdmans Books for Young Readers, 2016), 128–130.

Many do not achieve that purpose in their lifetime, and depart with a sense of work left undone. Sometimes this results from a lack of courage, sometimes from mistaken assumptions about what one is called to do. There are many other reasons, including accidents and violence, that I can neither enumerate nor understand. But it is because someone may think his calling is to be a writer, and end up a mediocre one, when his real gift was for jazz trumpet, fatherhood, architecture, or government, that I cannot say that everyone ought to become a writer. The skill of writing clearly is well worth acquiring, if only for the sake of lucid thought, but not everyone is called to write and publish books.

If we listen to the still small voice that speaks from our innermost being, more through a sense of peace than through audible speech, and if we follow its leading, we will go where we need to go. Eventually we discover that we are entangled in a polyphonic music, adding our individual harmony, melody, countermelody, or basso ostinato to the whole. Our participation, our contribution to that music, results in a richer and lovelier performance than any individual could do from her own strength and ability, in the same way that a large ensemble of different instruments, whether symphonic orchestra or gamelan, produces a complexity and depth of sound that cannot be achieved by one oboe or one kettledrum.

That music began long before our entrance and will

continue after we have played our final note. Nevertheless, every part, however brief or simple, is important. If the composer's score requires the triangle to play only two notes at the very end, and those notes are missed, something crucial is lost.

This is a picture of the kingdom of God, with all creation singing hymns of praise to the Creator. "All the earth worships you and sings praises to you; they sing praises to your name" (Ps. 66:4).[35] The instruments and singers include not only violins, trumpets, and cymbals but the sun, the moon, the stars, the wind in the trees, the whales in the sea, the hum of bees, the rain that falls. Many of us, if we are fortunate, have heard snatches of this song in passing: when we see October leaves gilded by a streetlight against a rich blue sky, for example, or a lake turned to a silver candle by the reflection of the sun.

In this picture, God the Father is the composer, who planned the piece from the beginning. The Holy Spirit conducts us, coordinating our separate parts for the beauty of the whole. Christ is the living tree cut down for its maple flame and the silver ore smelted for its sweetness of sound, through whom we make our music. Where then are we?

The present state of Christianity might be said to resemble a rehearsal room full of toppled chairs and music stands, where a determined clarinetist and two violas are

---

35. See also Psalms 19, 66, 96, and 148, or Isaiah 55:12, or the Benedicite Omnia Opera.

trying to follow the conductor's baton. In the back of the room, ignoring the conductor, a marimba player bangs out the latest pop hit. Meanwhile, a hundred violinists are brawling in the hall.

Sixty of those violinists should have been variously trained on viola, cello, double bass, bassoon, piccolo, tuba, trombone, French horn, and the other instruments that the composer calls for in his work, but the other violinists dissuaded them. There is only one acceptable role in the orchestra, they insist, and that is to play the violin. The clarinetist and violas heard the claim, considered it, and rejected it, but the others believed the violinists, or else did what was easy and expected of them. And so the orchestra now is missing many parts and players. The music has strange silences in it. It will not be finished until those browbeaten into learning the wrong part, or mistaken in their choice, learn to play what they were called to play.

Anyone who has observed any group of Christians knows that the role of violin might stand for being a white middle-class American, a member of a specific denomination, a submissive housewife, or an adherent of a specific creed. Orchestras do need many violins. But when the violins decide that, since they form a majority, they alone are acceptable and worthy before God, and everyone else ought to be exactly like them, they cause divisions, schisms, inquisitions, and other periodic outbreaks of sectarian violins.

Imagine the kind of faith, the constant looking to the Conductor, the strength of character, and the endurance needed for a percussionist in such an orchestra to learn what the role asks of him: to wait thirty or fifty or a hundred fifty measures of rest, and at the right moment, eyes never leaving the baton, to strike the two notes on a triangle that complete the praise song of the universe.

The task should not be so daunting, but in the present, we have made it so.

The percussionist need not admire the second trumpet or share his political or theological opinions in order for them to play their respective parts well. All that is asked is that both obey the Conductor and respect the music. It is best if they love the music and each other, but one can love and care for the good of another without liking him. That is better than the other way around.

If this illustration is too fanciful, consider instead a General in command of an army. He assigns two or twelve soldiers to the role of scouts or spies (Numbers 13 and Joshua 2). These two or twelve are separated from the main body of fighters and given an entirely different mission. What happens to the General's battle plans if those scouts choose to remain with the majority and perform the same tasks as the rest? If the army is disciplined, the other soldiers will encourage the scouts to carry out their orders, so the General's purpose can be accomplished. But if the army is undisciplined and unfamiliar with the

General's intentions, the majority may discourage those with different marching orders, or even fall upon them with accusations of treachery.

There are, and have always been, Christians who punish and persecute their fellow Christians as ferociously as the authorities in countries where Christianity is proscribed. They boast about what they do and say it pleases God. But the magnitude of their ignorance is such that they would not recognize their General if He walked through their midst. As a result, many battles are lost that should have been won, because a particular person was not in the right place at the right time, or else was hindered from his task.

As a minor example of the sort of assignment I mean, I once dealt with such at a summer Bible school. The adults who were serving were instructed to end the talks on time so the young people could break into groups for discussion. The small group time, we were told, was the most important part of the summer school. During one brother's message, I sat next to a nineteen-year-old who was serving for the first time, having only graduated from that summer school the previous year. The speaker went ten minutes over his assigned time, keeping us in our chairs and preventing us from splitting into groups. The young woman beside me glanced at the clock, then at the speaker, shifted in her chair, and glanced back at the clock.

It was obvious that she had taken our instructions to heart. I was not as bothered, having long become inured to male monologues. But her agitation was visible and intensifying.

You don't want me to do anything, do you, Lord? I said silently.

Raise your hand, came the reply.

Absolutely not.

Raise your hand.

But I don't care that he's going over.

Raise your hand.

I laid one hand on the young woman's arm to quiet her and raised my other hand. The brother who was speaking did not notice. I waved. He remained oblivious. Although his eyes were open, he did not see the clock, the restless audience, or my gesticulations. More minutes ticked by.

Finally I said, "Brother? I think it's time to go to small group."

And we did.

Later, when we went down for dinner, another woman confronted me.

"I just wanted to say," she said, "that I felt *very uncomfortable* when you interrupted that brother."

I said, "Sometimes we feel uncomfortable because someone has done something against God. Sometimes we feel uncomfortable because someone is not acting according to social conventions and hierarchies. Ask God how He sees the situation."

"I just wanted to tell you that I felt uncomfortable," she said.

"Ask God how He feels," I said.

I took a plate of food and sat at the end of the table, several empty seats from anyone else, and ate in silence, grieved. I had done as God asked, I had disregarded hierarchy and social niceties, and I had been rebuked for it.

After dinner, the woman who had criticized me found me again.

"Sister," she said, an odd look on her face, "God has given you a special gift."

He had given orders, rather. I didn't like them. But I had obeyed. I bless that woman for being willing to ask God for His view of things; very few people convinced of their own righteousness are able to do so.

Afterward, I approached the brother I had interrupted and explained the instructions the serving ones had received in the preparatory meeting that he had not attended.

He said, obtuse, "I accept your apology."

I said gently, "It was not an apology."

Understanding only came after obedience, as MacDonald said. If I had not intervened, the nineteen-year-old would have interrupted the brother, would have been chastised, and would not have been able to respond as I had. It is possible that the experience would have driven her out of the church entirely, if not embittered her toward Christianity as a whole. I was used to prevent that sequence of events. The task had been an unpleasant and lonely one, but once I understood its purpose, I was glad I had obeyed.

A few years later, after much prayer, I would leave that church, which I had grown up in, to be useful as Noah's ravens were useful, whose departure without return provided Noah with information. It did not matter, in the end, what anyone there thought of me. But it is likely that what they thought of that young woman matters still.

When I can find both time and practice space, which is not often, I take up my flute and play. But in this other, greater orchestra, where the parts are many but the musicians few, when the Conductor points to the triangle and indicates that I must play it, on His beat, whatever I feel or think about the situation, or about triangles, I pick it up and I do.

Chapter Four

CRAFT

THERE IS A FISHHOOK OF AN INVITATION OR QUESTION — the form is variable — that is regularly dangled in front of me in ambiguous or challenging contexts, that will hook and tear through the soft inside of my cheek if I bite.

"Tell me what to do."

I decline to respond. Whether it concerns an emerging technology or foreign policy or writing advice, the barb lies in the question's transferal of all responsibility, which every human being is meant to bear for himself, from asker to asked. If I give a perfect answer, and the asker carries it out, however beneficial the outcome, the asker is then left in the same situation as before, without having grown, without having decided upon an action for himself, and without bearing the responsibility and consequences for that decision. Again the asker says, as helpless as before, "Okay, *now* what do I do?"

But if my answer is imperfect or incorrect, or the asker only does things halfheartedly, and the results are poor, the asker can declare, "It's not my fault. I did what I was told, and it didn't work. It's the fault of the person who told me what to do."[1]

What we have forgotten is that, past maturity, no one but God can rightly say what any human being ought to do in the labyrinth of decisions that make up a single day. That is an intimate and private conversation between spirit and Spirit, if we choose to have it. No one else can have that conversation in our place. We can ask wise people for advice, and improve our knowledge of the problem space, though sometimes advice and knowledge can be debilitating. But in the end the individual must weigh all suggestions, knowledge, and even divine command within herself, against her conscience, intuition, and reason,[2] and

---

1. I suspect that this insistence on occupying a child's role, including the complete abdication of personal responsibility while retaining the right to blame others, has destroyed tens of thousands of marriages.
2. Not rationalization, which is the unconscious self-justification of our choices, but clear and disciplined thought.

decide what she will do. By choosing, she grasps her own life in her hands and makes herself.

Questions that do not shirk responsibility, that do not try to extend one's childhood, sound like these: What books have you found useful for a writer's development? What questions could people ask themselves about this situation? What do people forget to consider?

I am glad to answer them.

Those who demand certainty and security have not yet learned that, as Helen Keller wrote, "Security is mostly a superstition" experienced neither by animals nor by God, who entrusted His creation to the care of human beings. "Life," she says, "is either a daring adventure or nothing."[3] Nothing is certain, no one is secure, and everything has to be risked, sooner or later, for a greater good. There is no prescription or protocol that, if followed, guarantees artistic success. Unlike an engineer, a doctor, or an astronaut, who can follow established paths, receive widely recognized credentials, and seek placement in a pool of existing jobs,[4] the artist wanders into the same dark woods as Dante and becomes lost. Occasionally he may find himself in a sunlit clearing, or experience a sense of arrival, of being where he is meant to be, often at a point of real

---

3. Helen Keller, *Let Us Have Faith* (New York: Doubleday, Doran & Co, 1940), 50–51. Also from that passage: "Faith alone defends."
4. This is not to say that all members of these professions take the same paths, only that those paths exist.

personal accomplishment. This may not correspond to any degree of external recognition. But while he has certainly begun somewhere else and come by some route to that place, nothing more permanent than breadcrumbs marked his wandering, and no other artist can take the same path. Every artist must plunge into the thicket and find his own way. I am not sure that the lifelong artist ever emerges for more than a moment, blinking at the sunlight, the cultivated fields, the smokestacks and chimneys of the civilized world, before turning back into the trees. The point is to make a home in wild mystery.

The irreproducible life of the individual artist is that one artist's curriculum and path. No one else can profitably copy it. One writer enrolls in a writing program and earns a degree; another works a series of jobs; a third goes to war. Each one gains a specific set of experiences and skills that, one way or another, are integrated in the writer's being and put to use. Their writing will be as rich and varied as their lives have been. Literature would be drab and monotonous indeed if only one kind of person with one set of experiences wrote one type of book.

Whatever the path taken, temptations, ambiguity, obstacles, doubt, and despair will arise in every person's life. If artists have one advantage, it is that these afflictions tend to arrive sooner. However badly or well we handle them, if we leave past hardships to the effects of time, sun, wind, and rain, rather than preserving them under glass, over time they will break down into a fertile soil that nourishes our work. If artists have a second advantage in this regard, it is a disposition to creativity, which when wielded in the darkest situations can serve as a pickax in a gold mine.

In spite of the uncertainty, risk, and idiosyncrasies of the artist's individual path, writers over the centuries have generally agreed upon a number of skills and principles that are core to the craft. I will lay some of them out briefly, along with what I know, and the books that I have found most helpful. The reader may take what is useful and leave the rest.

LANGUAGE

The first of these, critical to poets and still necessary for novelists, is a deep love of language inextricable from a love of truth. These loves must be, but are not always, entwined with a love of life and growth. Subtract the love of life, subtract the vitality, and the result is Mervyn Peake's *Titus Groan* or Julio Cortázar's *Hopscotch*, which are crystalline wonders more architectural than alive. Keep vitality, and what comes forth from the love of language warms and stirs the reader to life.

W. H. Auden describes the poet as marrying language in order to beget the poem.[5] The degree of intimacy, the

---

5. In a private conversation with Rollo May, recounted in May, *The Courage to Create*, 85. A similar sentiment is expressed in W. H. Auden's essay

type of the love between writer and language, is spousal. It is not the instrumental or utilitarian love of money, power, or ice cream, more properly called cupidity, which spends, consumes, and uses the object for various other ends. To love language for itself, one must understand and uphold its purpose, which is to describe, grasp, or intensify the real, and by so doing bridge the distance between any two people. Like any other love, it can be both serious and silly. The playful and delightful hapaxes in Ogden Nash's light verse, comprehensible even though they exist nowhere else, are a sign of such a love.

This requirement alone disqualifies many of those writing and publishing today from the name of artist, though some may be making useful, pleasant, and entertaining works. There will always be a place for and interest in whatever is written without the deep love of language, if it has other consolations. That class of work, being more accessible, is, in fact, usually more popular. But it lacks the fineness and acuity of vision that can, with a word, pierce the veils of perception and let a startling light fall through.

Multilingualism

Like any mature and genuine love, the love of language calls for a lifetime's exploration of the beloved. This used to be better known. "Anybody who loves language,"

"Writing," but in terms of racehorse parentage. Auden, *The Dyer's Hand* (New York: Vintage International, 1989), 22.

Auden wrote, "knows that he cannot fully understand his mother-tongue without a working knowledge of at least two other languages, just as one cannot understand one's mother country without having lived in at least two others."[6] Although Auden's claim may sound outrageous to those of us in the present, it is only in the past century or so that monolingualism became common in English-speaking countries.

In the 1300s, in Chaucer's England, the preferred languages of government and literature were French and Latin. The educated citizens called *clerkes*, whose descendants are surnamed Clark, knew Latin and often French as well. European scientists were Latinists until the late nineteenth century. Benjamin Franklin knew French, Italian, Spanish, and Latin; Thomas Jefferson knew these four and also Greek. Of the first ten American presidents, eight were multilingual, and Martin Van Buren's first language was Dutch. The exceptions were George Washington and Andrew Jackson.

Fluency in multiple languages was a prerequisite for university admissions. Harvard required Latin, Greek, French, and German. In 1886, this standard was relaxed to allow the substitution of mathematics or science for Latin or Greek. Dismayed by this change in policy, school

---

6. "Words and the Word" in *Secondary Worlds: Essays by W. H. Auden* (New York: Random House, 1968), 140.

principal James Jay Greenough defended the classical languages in *The Atlantic*, writing:

> Being thus obliged to look at each thought from two points of view, the Latin or Greek and the English, he [the student] is forced to get a clearer conception of the thought than he could possibly get by looking at it from the English side only. As few words in two widely different languages have exactly corresponding conceptions behind them, — that is, are synonyms, — he must get at these conceptions to see what a sentence really means. He must think, and think clearly. He grows accustomed to clear thinking, and therefore expresses his own thoughts more clearly both in speech and in writing.[7]

To write clearly is to think clearly, as numerous writers after Greenough have also asserted. Both require rounds of revision, clarification, interrogation, and integration. Revising her writing, the writer revises her thinking as well, and learns to leave open the possibility of a better thought or a better expression of that thought. Studying a language dissimilar to one's mother tongue produces the same salubrious effects, but more rapidly, due to the greater contrast between what one says and intends.

---

7. James Jay Greenough, "The Present Requirements for Admission to Harvard College," *The Atlantic* (May 1892), 673–674, https://cdn.theatlantic.com/media/archives/1892/05/69-415/132122854.pdf.

What is most valuable is not any specific language but the struggle to apprehend the different and distinct worldview encoded in a language not one's own: how the radicals in Chinese, such as water, fire, or wood, convey some degree of semantic meaning even when the word is unknown; how Egyptian hieroglyphs are read into the faces of human and animal figures, but otherwise may run in any direction, and how much of it is titular and liturgical boilerplate; how Persian absorbs both French and Arabic words with cosmopolitan ease, so that both Parisians and Iranians go about saying *merci* in identical situations. Odd commonalities and points of interest appear: one cannot say "goodbye" in English or Persian without invoking God; *procrastinator* is literally "someone who for-tomorrows"; Italian's vowel-ended profligacy with rhymes, wherein far more words fall into fewer buckets than in English, might explain why the Shakespearean sonnet permits as many as seven different rhymes, while the Petrarchan sonnet permits only four or five. The greater the divergence of the new language from the learner's first language, the greater the difficulty of acquisition and the corresponding reward.

Anyone who has learned English as a second, third, or fourth language, to the point of appreciating and analyzing English literature, especially poetry, has in the course of their studies already learned to think through the construction of a sentence in multiple languages. The gift I describe, a readiness to grapple with words to achieve the best and clearest expression of meaning, is already theirs.

While Latin and Greek are not required for clarity in thinking and writing, their benefit to writers working in English is an automatic awareness of the etymologies of a large number of English words, particularly if combined with French and German. Access to the roots of words allows for more thorough and extensive work with language, in the same way that a gardener who is permitted to excavate the roots of plants and shrubs is capable of more radical plantings and arrangements than if he were limited to surface leaves and flowers.

Precision

A sound grasp of etymology and shades of meaning allows for precision and correctness in writing. To use the right word at the right moment is to drive a nail home, fixing the work to reality. The careful study and application of language gives the writer the power to not only depict reality accurately, which is rare enough, but also to use reality itself as the medium and material — to paint with reality. The names of the watercolors I carry around, adding to them now and then, are not fanciful, imagined terms, but accurate labels of the contents. My fingernail-sized box of ocher paint has ocher in it; someone in fact burned some umber for that brown; zinc white contains the same zinc oxide as sunscreen; bone black is made with charred animal bone.

To know that the black on my brush and page is bone char, to know that the stroke of paint I put down echoes through studios and scriptoria to soot-traced handprints on cave walls, reminds me of my place in history, in art, and in the physical world. Vermeer used bone black for *Girl with a Pearl Earring*; Rembrandt's portraits are shadowy with it.

To be correct and precise with language means either having the right word prepared and ready, or being willing to hunt for it through technical glossaries, visual dictionaries, and labeled diagrams of every kind. It means sifting through paper thesauri until the exact shade of meaning is found. The work can be wearying, but as Mark Twain famously remarked, the right word is as different from the almost-right word as lightning is from a lightning bug.

As one example of bottled lightning, Frederick Buechner offers a line from Gerard Manley Hopkins' remembrance of a farrier, who "didst fettle for the great gray drayhorse his bright and battering sandal." Hopkins' careful choice of words for their sound and clarity awakens in us, Buechner says, "a sense of the uniqueness and mystery and holiness not just of the blacksmith and his great gray drayhorse, but of reality itself, including the reality of ourselves."[8] We are more alive for having read the line,

---

8. Frederick Buechner, *The Sacred Journey: A Memoir of Early Days* (New York: HarperOne, 1982), 68.

as is the drayhorse, and for a brief moment, like the after-image that lightning leaves upon the eyes, the late Felix Spencer, the farrier in the poem, is present to us as well.

Used rightly, language hallows. It concentrates life and attention to life, reminds us of what is holy, and leaves us alert, awake, and startled by the wonder of the world and the word: by the colors in the visible spectrum and the word-hoard alike; by the distances between words, far apart as stars or close as atoms in a crystal; by the endless shades of difference between one leaf and the next, or one word and the next.

Used badly, however, language can deaden, dull, and anesthetize. The very worst abuses, usually committed by politicians and marketing agencies, not only fail to affix meaning to reality, but drive a wedge between them. The result is an overall falsification of the language that others rely on to say true things. I know no other word for this than desecration. Political language, Orwell reminds us, "is designed to make lies sound truthful and murder respectable, and to give an appearance of solidity to pure wind."[9]

The writer who strives for fresh and living language rooted in reality, the kind of language that awakens us to the world and each other and God's glory in both,[10] ful-

---

9. George Orwell, "Politics and the English Language."
10. See Hopkins' "Pied Beauty," with its exultant "Glory be to God for dappled things."

fills, in her sometimes lonely, always solitary work, the offices of a holy priesthood.

TECHNIQUE

The skills gathered under the heading of technique are, in aggregate, of equal importance to a mastery of language. A novelist without a complete mastery of language can succeed with perfect technique, but a poet lacking mastery of language cannot compensate in the same way. Technique includes a sense of a story's tension, as of a wire in a gauge, and the handling of narrative exigencies and their resolutions so that the wire is drawn out evenly and gains strength. It includes a careful handling of point of view and time and space, so that the reader is not jolted back and forth between three brains every other sentence, or between thirty planets in the course of a chapter, or accidentally given knowledge private to one character while occupying the perspective of another. Fortunately, technique is far more commonly taught and discussed than other aspects of writing I address in this book. I will add a few observations below, but these are the guides I have found most instructive:

Aristotle, *Poetics*
John Gardner, *The Art of Fiction*
Ursula K. Le Guin, *Steering the Craft*

Lajos Egri, *The Art of Dramatic Writing*
Donald Maass, *Writing 21st Century Fiction*
Renni Browne and Dave King, *Self-Editing for Fiction Writers*

Plot

In the common understanding, which I believe to be a misunderstanding, the word *plot* denotes the events that happen in a story, including at least one major conflict and resolution. But I consider events to be plot only if they arise naturally out of unavoidable tensions between one character's personality, needs, and deepest desires and those of another character; between contradictory needs and desires within a single character; or between those desires and the obstructive forces of the world that the character inhabits, including laws of nature and divinity, if present. Anything that exceeds this naturalness smacks of melodrama, deus ex machina, or carelessness and lack of skill. Rather than plot, it may be better to speak of the bones of a story, or its internal architecture, which suggest form and wholeness, as well as the creation and design of the story toward a particular end.[11]

---

11. Kishōtenketsu is said to be plotless, by the common understanding of plot, but it still requires the internal tensions I have described above to stand, much in the way that the stones of an arch press against each other.

Writers who suppose plot to be any sequence of events whatsoever, as long as obstacles appear, often fling their characters through disconnected encounters and episodes that resemble a miniature golf course, placing a windmill here, a ramp there, with little of the world or its real constraints persisting from moment to moment, and somewhat artificial stakes. An apartment building is flung up in one paragraph and blasted apart in the next to prove that a villain is evil, but while body parts and blood fly about, the reader does not care, because the writer also does not believe in the existence and permanence of that building or its residents. Were it otherwise, the writer would have shown that building early on, introducing several of its residents and establishing its history and materiality, long before it was sacrificed to make a point. The world would have been constructed so that there was a reason for that specific building to meet an explosive end, rather than any of a number of alternatives. Both its construction and destruction should have been costly to the author. By laying a careful foundation beforehand, in the way I have described, even surprising and shocking events can be made to appear natural and inevitable in hindsight.

Whatever does not appear so should be cut away, or else the entire work rewoven until it is whole and smooth. The problem for the author is not how to construct exciting adventures to be imposed upon a cast of characters, but how to construct a planet whose tectonic forces lift up a range of mountains of such steepness and altitude that the accidental discharge of a musket by a member of the Royal Guard precipitates an avalanche that buries the king's carriage and thereby begins a war. It includes deriving and developing the character of the unfortunate guard, and those who judge and sentence him, and the effects of that death, war, and sentence upon whatever economic, political, and legal systems are at play. This is all done so that when the novel begins two generations later, the stain of familial shame, and a hunger for redemption, will naturally emerge in that guard's granddaughter and drive her forward, through a landscape still scarred in places by that war, into encounters with people with their own painful memories from that time, their own histories, and the resultant cruelties, reactions, and moments of overflowing grace.

It is rare for a writer to be able to work everything out before beginning to write. There is much doubling back, revision, correction, reconstruction, and often revelation. But by the time the book is complete, the writer must know causes and effects, must grasp the laws and possibilities and materiality of the world, and must intuit the personal and family histories that influence individual characters' experiences of the present, not simply for the richness and texture these evoke, but because this is how a human being, a family, or a city is formed. We only create a sense of real life and liveliness when we imitate not just appearances but the natural processes of the world, although little of this work will reach the surface.

To hold the reader's interest over the course of a novel, regardless of specific story structure, successive tensions and conflicts must be, on average, of higher emotional intensity than those that came before, whether that emotion is anger, fear, or delight, until shortly before the end. It is for this reason that characters must have unavoidable tensions and conflicts with themselves, others, and the world, many of which cannot be resolved except to the detriment of one party. A glider's rubber band must be wound tightly at launch to drive the glider as far as it has to go. If it falls short, the band can be wound more tightly, or the entire glider redesigned and rebuilt, until that degree of propulsion is achieved. In the same way, characters and encounters in a first draft that falls short, which is almost every first draft, are questioned and inspected until they yield additional sources of tension and conflict. That tension must then be traced backwards through history until a potential origin is discerned, at which point the world is rebuilt so that it becomes an inevitability.

The second draft may fly a little farther. Again the glider is dismantled and rebuilt, wound up and launched. The process continues until finally glider or novel crosses that span under its own power, delicate and inexorable in its operation as a physical law. The heart sings at that sight.

Variation and Proportionality

Bathos is deadly. I have laughed, as Twain's Joan of Arc laughed, as many people will laugh, at serious and earnest stories badly told. At the same time, I know that I cannot make any reader cry without first making her laugh. Nor can I reveal anything of worth directly without it losing both its value and its power.[12] If the writer is to convey any kind of deep truth about life, however beautiful or painful, she must "walk the reader to the guillotine without his knowing it," as Baldwin says.[13]

That requires a kind of fascination or entrancement, which only variety and contrast can sustain.[14] Consider the immense variation in mood and tone in any symphony or oratorio, whether Rimsky-Korsakov's hour-long *Scheherazade* or Bach's three-hour *St. Matthew Passion*, that is required to hold the listener rapt. Reading a novel takes much longer, and requires at least as much color and invention, as much contrast and change. Rare is the person who can sit motionless through an hour-long dirge or dance a two-hour polka without dropping dead.

For the sake of believability, outside of parody and farce, the writer should attach only as much significance to objects and events as they can bear, or provide additional

---

12. The gift of revelation is reserved to God.

13. James Baldwin, "Words of a Native Son," in *The Price of the Ticket: Collected Nonfiction, 1948–1985* (Boston: Beacon Press, 2021), 403.

14. "Age cannot wither her, nor custom stale / Her infinite variety," Shakespeare's Mark Antony says of Cleopatra.

scaffolding for the extra weight. Some things, like hippos, gelatin desserts, and pizza bagels, cannot bear very much seriousness or preaching. Unless the point is a Popean satire upon the frivolousness of society, or a portrait of a disordered personality, a chipped acrylic nail should not be treated as equivalent to an eviction, or a schoolyard threat to annihilation. This presumes common sense in both reader and writer. Although those who are willing and able to determine the proportionality or disproportionality of their own and others' reactions and responses seem to be a diminishing population, some still remain. It is preferable and courteous to assume a sane and sensible audience, and write with that ideal reader in mind.

Character

In terms of technique, character is a shorthand reference to some combination of psychological insight, understanding of human behavior, and the ability to construct a coherent or at least plausible individual personality. Those personalities must be compelling enough to hold the reader's interest for the length of the story or novel. The longer the work, the more compelling the characters must be. As with plot, the problem is not one of patchwork and piecemeal construction, but of building a whole life, with all that this entails. Books written without a sufficient grasp of character substitute cardboard cutouts, stock characters recognizable from other books and films, rigid masks that do not reveal the slightest degree of humanity, and lightly disguised switches and levers that exist only to shunt the plot this way and that.

While the writer with sufficient self-awareness, who has observed himself carefully and can give a fair account of his strengths and weaknesses, has always one character to draw upon, no writer can do more than this without stepping into the mass of humanity and having real and often bruising encounters there. Characters borrowed from other books tend to be recognized. The creation of characters who appear to live and react and move as living people do requires close attention to how human beings speak and act in diverse contexts and toward very different people.

The same man responding to the same stimulus, say someone stepping on his foot, is likely to say different things depending on whether the person who has trod upon him is wealthy, poor, old, young, clumsy, aggressive, male, or female, and depending on whether he is at a restaurant where he waits tables, at an investment firm he oversees, at home with his family, in the middle of a mob of fellow soccer fans, or on the front lines of a bitter and protracted battle. Insights from psychology, such as the unconscious defense mechanisms described by Anna Freud, organizational psychology's studies of group decision-making processes and the prestige and dominance models of leadership, or Eric Berne's model of transactional analysis, can be useful in systematizing these observations and predicting others, but they cannot replace individual observation, attention, and investigation.

The problem of character will be developed further in the last third of this book.

Subtext

The writer who believes that personally experiencing strong emotions while writing, or baldly describing emotion on the page, is sufficient to move the reader, has not yet learned the ineffectiveness and irrelevance of both of these things. It takes subtlety, understatement, and long and careful preparation, including submerging meaning beneath surface words and acts, to lure the reader into the writer's trap. These matters are best accomplished in a sober frame of mind.

The unskilled writer has every character cry as a universal indicator of sadness and say "How could you hurt me?" to communicate a sense of hurt. Readers who have seen this hundreds of times before are unlikely to be affected. The skilled writer has a character who has long prided herself on tidiness, who gives tours of her home, who is regularly complimented on her housekeeping, leave off cleaning until the mirror grows speckled and the carpet gritty. This individual and private expression of sadness is far more powerful in effect, though no visible tears are shed.

Alternatively, say that a character is considering suicide. The situation is serious but easily mishandled. "I can't take it anymore!" a stock character yelps, drawing a knife. "I'm going to kill myself!" And the reader yawns, because this is the rattling of a cardboard-and-tinfoil saber, and nothing is truly at stake. Even if the character is puppeted through the act, and falls a corpse upon the stage, the reader knows that the death was faked, because that character was never alive.

"I'm sorry, I won't be able to make it," a living character says in response to a close friend's wedding invitation. "I won't be around." Perhaps she hangs up the phone and lightly crosses out all the days on the calendar after Tuesday. The reader who has noted her understated responses to the small humiliations of daily life, and her acts of love and care for that friend, if these things have been planted throughout the novel, may realize the significance of her words and experience real dread. He has received a key to her character that allows him to infer the underlying extremities of emotion.

This is subtext, or the caching of meaning for the reader to unearth. Outside of fiction, subtext is often used for covert aggression and the delivery of vicious cuts beneath a veneer of niceness: "Wow, it's very brave of you to wear that," for example. Inside of fiction, if the writer and reader are both careful and thoughtful, this burying and unburying becomes a form of collaborative play, surprising and delighting the reader. It also has a good chance of evoking in the reader the intended emotional response. Since subtext assumes intelligence and discernment, it is a gesture of respect from writer to reader, and is often repaid in attentiveness.

❧

It is easy enough to name these elements of craft. It is hard to learn them, harder to apply them well, and hardest to practice them so thoroughly and for so long that language and technique become absorbed by the intuition, integrated into the artist's being, and thereafter remain invisible and unconscious, but ready to hand. This absorption requires a period of dedication to learning and practicing the craft, not to be confused with a formal degree program,[15] and much solitary study, trial, and failure. To give a sense of the duration of the apprenticeship, several writers have suggested that the beginner does not produce competent work before writing and discarding a million words. This competence, which produces solid, serviceable journeyman work, is still not mastery, which lies much further along. Francis Thompson has noted that this long

---

15. It is certainly possible for this process to take place over the course of a degree program, but also possible for it to begin only after completing the program, for it to end prior to entry into the program, or for it to occur without any formal program whatsoever.

study of the living laws of Art or God is a process that saints and artists have in common:

[The Poet] absorbs the law into himself; or rather he is himself absorbed into the law, molded to it, until he become sensitively respondent to its faintest motion, as the spiritualized body to the soul. Thenceforth he needs no guidance from formal rule, having a more delicate rule within him. He is a law to himself, or indeed he is the law. In like manner does the Saint receive into himself and become one with divine law, whereafter he no longer needs to follow where the flocks have trodden, to keep the beaten track of rule; his will has undergone the heavenly magnetization by which it points always and unalterably towards God.[16]

The development of the mature artistic intuition described here is not a romantic ideal but a practical necessity. The writer's knowledge of the principles of craft, sensitivity toward language, and personal sensibility must be unified, must become a singleness, in the moment of creation and revision, if the work is to emerge as a unity. The entirety of the artist's attention must be fixed upon the work, watching for its direction of growth, and noticing the places where buds should be pruned back, or branches

---

16. Francis Thompson, *Health and Holiness* (London: J. Masters & Co, 1905), 37.

trained along a trellis, so that the work becomes what it must be. Overt consciousness of technique and precept destroys the artist's singular focus and fragments the work.

I suspect that the apprenticeship is as long and grueling as it is in order to teach us the worth of the gift we were given, so that we do not lose or sell or waste it. I think it entirely possible to lose, sell, or waste the gift, as Samson lost his strength and Esau his birthright. Because art enters the world through an artist's body and mind, any vice that damages the artist's body or mind, or that separates the artist from reality and his own humanity, will sooner or later damage or diminish his art. Microscope lenses and telescope mirrors suffer greatly from the smallest particle of grit or the slightest scratch, and the artist's powers of perception are often just as delicate. It is for this reason that Jacques Maritain says, on the subject of the artist's morality, that a writer can theoretically poison others without adverse effects upon his prose, but a writer who becomes addicted to drugs is likely to become a worse or less productive writer as a consequence.[17]

There are other ways to break the compact. Prostitution of the creative gift is a betrayal. By this I do not mean applying one's skills to commercial work for a day job, piecework, or freelance work, which is often necessary to survive. A practical grasp of business, the ability to read

---

17. Maritain, *Creative Intuition in Art and Poetry*, 45.

and negotiate contracts, a basic knowledge of accounting and taxes, and some trade or profession that keeps a roof overhead and food on the table have all served writers well throughout history. "Most of the very great poets have been not only sane, but extremely business-like," G. K. Chesterton writes.[18] Rather, I mean pricing and selling the quiet spirit whose whisperings are meant for the artist's own work. I mean altering a work of real art away from what it is meant to be in order to appeal to the least discriminating. Several artists interviewed for William Deresiewicz's *The Death of the Artist*, including a best-selling author of pop guides on creativity, describe selling off pieces of their deepest selves, or their artistic convictions, for a TED talk, a consultancy, corporate sales, or donations and support from online fans, and their subsequent regrets.

I know that for myself, having sharpened my tools to keenness, to use the gift given me to write outright lies, or to deliberately deceive, would be equivalent to dragging one's best knife edge downward through gravel. I do not avoid lying out of a desire to be virtuous, or because I am a good person. I avoid it because it is likely to damage or cause the loss of a core artistic faculty that comes with particular conditions. Other artists may detect similar constraints upon their art, which are faintly sensed, in the way

---

18. G. K. Chesterton, *Orthodoxy* (London: The Bodley Head, 1909), 27.

that one feels for furniture and walls in the dark, rather than issued as explicit injunctions. They are no less binding for that.

In this age of unrestrained commerce and self-indulgence, we have forgotten that such limits exist, and that such losses are possible. That forgetfulness is a disservice to the artist. Fairy tales and the Bible are far more honest in this regard. They remind us, and warn us, that it is possible to trade one's voice for long legs and a chance at a prince, one's firstborn for a fistful of rampion, one's strength and sight for an end to unending questions, one's birthright for pottage, and Truth and Life for thirty pieces of silver. But if we have sweated, studied, labored, and suffered to master the craft, if we honor what has been given to us, and if we consider proper source and orientation in all things, then when temptation comes sweetly, as it always will, whatever we are offered in exchange for this gift will then correctly appear too dear.

Chapter Five

INSPIRATION

CALL IT INSPIRATION, OR THE SPIRIT BLOWING WHERE it lists, or white fire, or tongues of flame. Call it divine madness, as Plato does. But what remains constant across the ages, with the possible exception of our present age of omphaloskepsis, is how frequently artists and poets, and those who observe them at work, describe a force that originates outside of the artist and flows through her into the painting or poem. It is a grace poured out, a divine touch that may also lame us. An artist must have humility to give way to that force, as well as to acknowledge its part in her work. There is something more honest in Homer's ageless invocation, "Sing, O Muse," than in Whitman's "I sing myself," despite the energy and vivacity of Whitman's poem.

A gift is defined by its alterity. Someone other than the self, with the freedom to give or withhold, chooses whether to bestow it. Gifts, like grace, are maddeningly outside of our control. The artist prepares, invites, waits, prays, pleads, holds vigil, but does not demand inspiration and cannot compel it. The result of coercion in art, as in all matters, is stiff and lifeless. We produce something like a bearskin with glass eyes and bared teeth, rather than the roaring, roaming, living creature it could have been.

I find that gratitude for the first blessing improves my chances at a second, as does wonder, openness, the emptiness of upturned hands, and the setting aside of my preconceptions. Writers who are not Christian are not normally taught to whisper "Thank you" to the spirit that leaves its gift, much less to pursue the giver. Still, I do not say thank you often enough. G. K. Chesterton said grace before writing or reading, "sketching, painting / Swimming, fencing, boxing, walking, playing, dancing..."[1] By gratitude I do not mean an outward performance or recitation for the benefit of an audience, but an inward response of delight and thankfulness when the hoped-for idea or solution appears.

---

1. Maisie Ward, *Gilbert Keith Chesterton* (New York: Sheed & Ward, 1944), 59.

On rare occasions, a story arrives seamless and whole. At different times, two short stories were sloughed off, perfectly formed, like cicada shells, from long-form projects I was working on.

Once, a story mugged me.

I had spread the pages of the first draft of my novel over the carpet of my studio apartment, which faced westward onto frequent rain clouds and rainbows. I had intended to spend the week revising the novel. But a story crept up on me and demanded, peremptory as a rusty knife at my throat, that I attend to it instead. Over the next five days I scribbled into a notebook a nightmare of a tale that I suspect was complete before I was ever aware that it existed. The story formed itself continuously with the line of my pen, so that I barely had time to ask who was who, or what happened next, before answers presented themselves. I changed very little while revising, which is unusual; my stories normally require four full drafts, with extensive alterations.

To this day I have the strong sense of having been used as the most immediate and convenient doorway through which that particular story could break into this world. It is both recognizably a work of mine and alien to me.

For these exceptional cases, the artist can only give thanks. There is joy and awe, and in that one case, fear, in this kind of flood, in the direct and palpable touch of the Creator's hand. More often I am required to toil, to think, to struggle, to search, to inquire and choose. But even in this, I am only the wine barrel in which a long fermentation occurs, and out of which the wine flows. When I am asked why I gave a character a certain background, or made a particular creative decision, I am generally baffled. I do not choose which grape varietals to plant, nor which slopes to plant them upon. I do not own the vineyards or cause the vines to grow. I simply receive the proportions of sweetness and pomace that come to me and let things work themselves out in effervescent obscurity.

If the author exerts too much control, Maritain says, the characters wind up as clockwork automatons. Exert too little, and the work has no unifying vision or purpose.[2] L'Engle, in *The Rock That Is Higher*, says: "Story is seldom true if we try to . . . make it go where we want it to go, rather than where the story itself wants to go. . . . We listen to the story, and must be willing to grow with it."[3] Whatever grows is alive.[4] It has its own structure, course, and end. It is possible to coax and bend a living story into a given shape, as a gardener espaliers a pear, but this requires an understanding of the story's natural direction of growth and attention to its requirements.

---

2. Maritain, *Creative Intuition in Art and Poetry*, 126.
3. L'Engle, *The Rock That Is Higher*, 203.
4. Besides crystalline and mineral structures.

The craft of fiction has much in common with the mystery and vitality of sowing seeds, of pupating, of gestating and giving birth. A story well told is more closely related to a fuchsia's drooping bloom, a Douglas fir, a belted conk, or a honey bee than Linnaeus might admit. Fiction is also a risk, as all life is. There is always the threat of blight, rot, or drought.

Nevertheless, though the result is uncertain, anyone who would grow a living story must undertake both the pleasant and unpleasant tasks necessary for that end, as the farmer commits to weeding, watering, covering against frost, harvesting, and threshing, not knowing if a hailstorm or plague of locusts will descend and lay those efforts to waste. "I planted, Apollos watered, but God gave the growth," Paul writes to the Corinthians (1 Cor. 3:6). The artist labors in similar fashion, all the while hoping for the breath of life to enter into the work. The work, meanwhile, sits expectant as a seed, at once quiescent and explosive with growth.

The work itself must lead the artist, and not the other way around. As L'Engle puts the matter, the work presents itself and declares, "Here I am, serve me."[5] The artist then has the free choice to serve or not to serve. This choice also lay before Lucifer. It lies before every Christian. We are able to act and create out of love because we are also

---

5. L'Engle, *Walking on Water*, 23.

able to shake our heads and walk away. We can graciously receive the gift because we can also refuse it. If we refuse, sometimes the task goes to someone else, and it is brought forth another way. Sometimes, I think, it is lost, and its portion of light lost, because the one who was put here to do it would not.[6] The harvest is plentiful but the workers are few.

I am, on many days, lazy, tired, mulish, or distracted, reluctant to serve as I ought. When the quiet voice within me asks me to write, I will instead read or eat or go for a stroll. I have lost paragraphs and pages by not listening, and thereby delayed the completion of several works. My home is cleanest when I am avoiding a writing deadline. But what is more important than these brief lapses is that I *have* learned to listen to that voice, and that, more often than not, I obey. I know that obedience to that leading brings startling rewards.

Late one winter afternoon, exhausted, I inquired of my spirit if I ought to take a nap, and was nudged to take a walk instead. I repeated the question several times, because I was reluctant to stir, and each time the answer

---

6. In this I partially disagree with Martha Graham's words to Agnes de Mille: "There is a vitality, a life force, a quickening that is translated through you into action...if you block it, it will never exist through any other medium; and be lost. The world will not have it." Though sometimes this is true, sometimes the world does have the gift, through ways I cannot begin to understand. Agnes de Mille, *Martha: The Life and Work of Martha Graham* (New York: Random House, 1991), 264.

was the same. At the speed of molasses, I oozed off the sofa and out the door.

A mile from home, I was heading up an asphalt footpath between leafless shrubs of redcurrant, blackberry, and thimbleberry when, hardly a yard from me, a tawny feline dashed across the path and disappeared into the thicket on the other side. No one else was nearby. *Housecat*, I thought, blinking, then realized that I had seen black-tufted ears and a short tail tipped in white and black, and that I had never seen a housecat of that size. It was the local bobcat, which I had first spotted at a distance several months earlier, when other people pointed it out to me. Stepping between bushes, I saw its ringed tail and rabbit-colored haunches as it slunk away through the underbrush.

That encounter paints in miniature what I know of being inspired. Cheerfully or not, we obey the inner leading, walking however far, learning whatever subjects, or speaking whatever words we are asked to walk and learn and speak. In so doing we are placed on a collision course with something we cannot predict and do not control, though we may recognize it, that blurs across our path, wild and alive, and leaves us stunned.

I could have declined the invitation. I could have taken the nap. I would not have known what gift I missed.

If we live in this way, obedient to and prepared for inspiration, as the artists have it, or by the Spirit, as the Christians have it, no act or word of ours, no matter how small, will be without meaning. Though our acts and words slip into the waters of time and are lost to sight, the ripples they produce move across the waters and lap against a shore yet unseen. A single fallen leaf feeds many living things, not least its own tree. To ask the right question heals the Fisher King. To bless bread and break it makes a memorial that outlasts empires.

It is rare to see the consequences of our obedience to Spirit or inspiration as quickly as I did that day. I do not expect to see the ramifications of many of my actions in my lifetime, though I hope to know some of them someday. But if we become aware of the reverberations of individual acts through the centuries, we are likely to move through our lives with greater care and more prayer. I am alive and educated today not least because my illiterate grandmother raised and sold piglets to send my mother away to school. Two hours' drive from a city in Inner Mongolia, there is a flourishing grove of willows that catches the morning light beneath their branches, more golden than St. Peter's in Rome, and to me more holy, because my mother helped plant them when she was a girl.

This is not romance, but contingency,[7] chance balanced on a knife's edge, falling this way or that. That I am alive is as improbable as a thousand dice rolls coming up all sixes, and might never have occurred, but for acts of generosity

---

7. Christian Wiman repeatedly associates Christ with contingency in *My Bright Abyss*, 16–20.

from people I never knew, and the determination of others in unthinkable circumstances, who had no idea that I would someday exist. I think the same is true of anyone else. I have no desire to elaborate upon the generations of suffering and sorrow that preceded me, or the suffering and sorrow that is to come; that is life, anyone's life. Some things are constant. But what astonishes me is how, here and there, a golden thread gleams out of the dark, stitching one remnant to another, until what has been lost and mourned is retrospectively altered in substance and form, so that something brighter emerges. We are promised that "all things work together for good, for those who are called according to his purpose" (Rom. 8:28). But how hard, sharp, and brilliant is that working for good, like a scalpel that wounds in order to heal. It does not stanch the flow of tears, though it changes them from tears of pain to tears of gratitude.

Seven years ago, when I was targeted at work by a woman known for scapegoating and a man known for sadism, I prayed with a longtime friend for a swift conclusion to the months of misery. "Resolve this situation quickly, O Lord," my friend said. God must love her dearly, because He listened. Two days later I was asked to resign from my job, which was not the outcome I had wanted. Less than a week later, my mother told me she was flying to China because my grandmother had been hospitalized. "Wait," I said. "I'm coming."

I found a $500 round-trip ticket from Seattle to Bei-jing for the Sunday after my last day at work, which I had never seen before and do not think I will ever see again. By plane, train, and car, I went with my mother to the hin-terlands, walked in the grove of trees she had planted, and spent several days with my grandmother, which was the last time I would see her alive. Although the experience was bitter and brutal for everyone, and I could not sleep because of a rat scrabbling among the rafters above me at night, I saw the hand of God in the arrangement of things, and I was grateful.

⌒

Where do I get my ideas—where does anyone get ideas? I read, observe, and write down whatever strikes me.[8] There are already far too many to realize in one lifetime, and more arrive every day. The notebook fills. I wait for a crit-ical mass of them, for a pressure to build, for promising combinations and cross-pollinations, ever listening, always ready to obey. Sometimes when I set out, the thread holds, my foot is sure, and the maze might as well be a straight path for all the obstruction it offers. At other times, like

---

8. Observing the natural world and human interactions and relationships, and reading nonfiction, scholarly papers, and older works, have been produc-tive for me. There are also parasitic writers who get their ideas from reading other writers' unpublished manuscripts and listening to their readings, one of whom informed me after I had read a story that he liked a turn of phrase so much, he was going to steal it. I consider that practice discourteous.

the faithful servant Julian of Norwich saw in one vision, who sets out eagerly to do the will of his lord, I promptly fall into a ditch.[9] *Six* ditches, in Karen Blixen's retelling of a pictorial story that she and I both heard as children, where the teller draws a line to illustrate the tale, adding a *V* for each time the protagonist falls in and climbs out. The man in the story may have been confused by the tremendous number of obstacles in his way, but he persisted. "He finished his course, he kept his faith," Blixen writes. "That man had his reward." When the sun rises and the long-suffering man looks out the window, he sees that his long night of struggle has traced the outline of a stork, its claws created by his repeated falls into ditches.[10] Along the same lines, Teresa of Ávila is supposed to have asked God, after slipping and falling during a river crossing, "When wilt thou cease from scattering obstacles in our path?" When the Lord responds, "It is ever thus that I treat My friends," she retorts, "It is also on that account that Thou hast so few!"[11]

An observer could easily conclude, based on the evidence, that the Christian life, or the inspired life, involves

---

9. Chapter 51 of *A Revelation of Love*. The following quotation is from Nicholas Watson and Jacqueline Jenkins, eds., *The Writings of Julian of Norwich* (University Park, PA: Penn State University Press, 2006), 275.

10. Karen Blixen as Isak Dinesen, *Out of Africa* (New York: Modern Library, 1992), 260–261.

11. *The Life of Saint Teresa*, trans. Alice Lady Lovat (London: Herbert & Daniel, 1912), 548. Probably apocryphal.

a lot of time spent lying at the bottom of ditches. That conclusion is correct. Julian's allegorical servant "groneth and moneth and walloweth and writheth," and Blixen passes on from her children's story to speak of "the dark pit in which I am now lying." Jonah is swallowed, Daniel shut up with lions, Joseph promoted from pit to prison. Before that, of course, he dreamed beautiful dreams.

To know the direction one is going, and the destination, and the appropriate time to set off, does not mean a safe journey. No one has any certainty, no one has any guarantee of safety, and yet the faithful ones go forth. The writer trusts the story and follows the glimmering thread. The Christian trusts the Author and Perfector and follows the pillar of cloud. However many pits and prisons they fall into along the way, they endure, they press onward, they chance their lives, they complete the story and find themselves somewhere new. But even if the morning does not bring a complete vision, even if success does not come before the grave, the One for whom we struggle watches our efforts, Julian says, with love and compassion, and "comforteth and socurreth...loving and longing to bring us to his blisse."[12]

There is no safety in this world, as Baldwin and L'Engle and Wiman remind us. The great service the writer performs for the world is reconciling us to that bitter fact, that

---

12. Watson and Jenkins, *The Writings of Julian of Norwich*, 276.

we may live in reality and with our eyes open. Art teaches us that safety is an illusion, and strengthens us to live without such illusions.[13] There is no safety in art, where the only certainty is protracted struggle; nor is there safety in Christianity, whose promise of resurrection presumes our deaths. That is not to say that one cannot choose, act, and speak wisely and thoughtfully, and in many cases mitigate risk and turn aside anger, but even the most perfect choices cannot protect us from war, accidents, natural disasters, or other human beings intent on harm. The end of every life is death and decay. Those who promise safety, rather than wise judgment and a sober willingness to bear responsibility, are at best ignorant, at worst deceptive. God does not promise safety but the pain of the cross, His love, and His eternal life, and whatever can be created out of these. That last promise, however, is nothing less than a universe.

Those who wish to be inspired must be willing to serve. Those who wish to be served will not find inspiration, or will find it, misuse it, and make a twisted work. Inspiration often leads us into ditches, pits, and lions' dens, demands all kinds of labor and obedience from us, and promises nothing in return. This is normal and to be expected, and many an artist has the scrapes, bruises, and scars to show for it. Very occasionally, that spirit affixes

13. Baldwin, "The Artist's Struggle for Integrity," in *The Cross of Redemption*, 51.

wings to our shoulders and teaches us to fly. And this is not to be expected, though it can be hoped for. But what it will never do is assure us of safety, comfort, or success. Whatever makes such promises is not real inspiration, does not come from the Spirit, and does not tell the truth. It is no honest guide; do not follow it.

Chapter Six

COURAGE

U NLIKE LIKEABILITY, POPULARITY, FAMILIARITY WITH alcohol, intimate personal disclosures, public performance of virtue, a good reputation, an online presence, or industry connections, all of which, in the end, can be done without, courage is fundamental to art. But courage is not discussed, sought after, or fretted over as often as the superficialities are, not least because it is a tectonic process, hidden until the revelation of tremor or eruption. Any work of art that transcends, any art that transforms and transfigures, at some point demanded more courage of the artist than the artist possessed, and had its demands met. "The only courage worth calling courage must necessarily mean that the soul passes a breaking point—and does not break," G. K. Chesterton writes.[1] One way or another, that artist reached and passed the crisis that Chesterton describes.

If an artwork is incandescent, then sufficient craft, love, and proper source and orientation are already present in the work. If it sets us on fire, we are partly responding to these things, but we are also responding to the exaltation and expansion of the artist's spirit in response to that demand for courage. To witness courage anywhere, in anyone, is to hear its calling to our own spirit.[2] If we accept that summons, if we allow the courageously created work of art to permeate our being and reconfigure us, then in some small way we share in that exaltation and expansion, and are not the same after.

Some art, at the critical moment, loses its nerve. We wince at the aborted attempt, as we might do when a beautiful thoroughbred that clears jump after jump with vigor and grace balks at the final fence. The desire was honorable and the craftsmanship sound, but the artist flinched, and a work that could have been deathless remains competent and mortal. The result is usually not a

---

1. G. K. Chesterton, *Orthodoxy* (London: Bodley Head, 1909), 256.
2. See, among many excellent works, Sandra Restrepo and Brené Brown, *The Call to Courage* (Netflix, 2019), and M. Scott Peck, *The Road Less Traveled* (New York: Simon & Schuster, 1978).

bad book but one near the top of its field. Yet it can evoke, like a silver medal, the thought: *If only...*

In an age that emphasizes images, performativity, and visibility over the invisible and intangible, courage tends to be misconceived. It is not the absence of fear but the refusal to be conquered and controlled by fear. It is not rash behavior but a mature willingness to reckon up and pay the costs of one's actions. It is not self-righteousness, with its sickly-sweet pleasures and sense of satisfaction, but a stomach-turning dread and lack of confidence that nevertheless produce right action. It is not inborn but accumulates over time through a gradual increase of the demands upon us.

The faces and forms of courage are too many to recount. It is not always recognized for what it is, even by the person who acts courageously. To hear God and obey is an act of courage; to tell the truth is another; to follow the story or artwork faithfully until the work is fully expressed is a third. It takes courage to love, to forgive, or to hold one's ground out of integrity. One can be courageous by being willing to be disliked, or by being willing to be happy.[3] The willingness to witness another's suffering and be impelled to do something about it, meanwhile, is what Rollo May calls perceptual courage.[4]

---

3. Ichiro Kishimi and Fumitake Koga, *The Courage to Be Disliked* (New York: Atria Books, 2018).
4. Rollo May, *The Courage to Create* (New York: W. W. Norton, 1975), 17.

Courage is not for eliciting recognition, admiration, and praise, but for causing us to become more deeply what we were created to be. It is a private and internal encounter first, before it develops external signs: Gethsemane before the cross. Its structure is self-referential and self-reinforcing, in that acting with courage prepares and strengthens each person for the next, more difficult trial. As we meet each test, we also encourage — that is, put heart into — those around us, and perhaps even those we do not yet see. Marianne Moore captures the paradoxical nature and counterintuitive effect of courage in her 1941 poem "What Are Years":

> ...And whence
> is courage: the unanswered question,
> the resolute doubt —
> dumbly calling, deafly listening — that
> in misfortune, even death,
> encourages others
> and in its defeat, stirs
>
> the soul to be strong?[5]

Even in its defeat, courage triumphs through its spiritual propagation into those who witness it, no matter how distant.

---

5. Marianne Moore, "What Are Years," in *The Complete Poems of Marianne Moore* (New York: Macmillan and Penguin, 1982), 95.

Almost a century later, I remain both haunted and guided by the words of Sophie Scholl, a member of the White Rose resistance group at the University of Munich, who along with her older brother was arrested for distributing anti-Nazi pamphlets. At the end of her trial for treason, in answer to a question, she said, "As before, and especially now, I'm convinced I did the best I could have done for my people. I don't regret my actions and I'm willing to shoulder the consequences that arise from my actions."[6] She, her brother Hans, and another White Rose member were convicted of treason, sentenced to death, and beheaded. Sophie was twenty-one. The year was 1943, two years after Moore's poem was published.

For me, any real demand for courage is accompanied by nausea, horror, anxiety, sleepless nights, and protestations to God, in hopes that the cup might be taken away. Luke 14:28–29 reminds us to tally up the construction costs of a tower before beginning the work, so that we are not disgraced by leaving it incomplete. Often I struggle to assent to what certain decisions may cost me, and wrestle with my soul through many nights before I am broken enough

---

6. Original: "Ich bin nach wie vor der Meinung, das Beste getan zu haben, was ich gerade jetzt für mein Volk tun konnte. Ich bereue deshalb meine Handlungsweise nicht und will die Folgen, die mir aus meiner Handlungsweise erwachsen, auf mich nehmen." Translated by Sabine Frost as a personal favor. Strafprozess gegen Hans Scholl u.a., Bundesarchiv Berlin, R 3017/34635, https://invenio.bundesarchiv.de/invenio /direktlink/21b35aa3-bbcc-4dd4-870a-fa85dcce9bb6.

to be able to say, "Your will be done." When I speak of costs, I do not mean exaggerated fears, but probabilistic assessments of worst, best, and intermediate outcomes. This too is part of courage. Acting without knowing or consenting to the consequences is not courageous but foolhardy. Most who behave in this way retract, renounce, or repudiate their actions when the costs become apparent, though one or two may find genuine courage in that moment, and pay what is asked without shrinking.

The degree of courage that is tested is relative to each individual. It is the difference between who one is and who one is asked to become. If we are lucky, the tests are incremental. I hesitate to provide examples from experience, first because I would sooner call myself fearful than courageous, and second because the courage demanded of me was far less than the courage demanded of any woman living in that country, both then and now. But because even my threadbare examples may be of use to those who are, as I am, not brave by nature, I will give them.

In my last year of college, while I was intensively researching a novel in between writing two theses,[7] I discovered that no matter how much I read about Afghanistan, where a short section of the novel took place, it was not enough for me to understand the texture of the

---

7. The novel had nothing to do with my coursework. With the benefit of hindsight, I might not have made the same decisions that I made then, but I am glad to have survived them.

country or to bring it to life. I mentioned my trouble to a guest speaker, who had some expertise in the area, and he listened to me and said, quite reasonably, "Then you'll have to go to Afghanistan." As I continued to research and write after graduation, I was increasingly confounded by this difficulty and by that imperative. I had visited detention centers in Australia and stepped onto a fishing boat in Jakarta without a second thought, but a war zone was something else altogether. Nevertheless, I was becoming aware that either I could do what the novel required of me, and go there and see things for myself, or I could refuse the risk and write that section of the novel based only on secondhand knowledge. Only in the first case would I have the chance to write something real and true. It was likely that no one else would know my decision, and possible that no one would blame me if it were known, but I would know. The work would know.[8]

To prepare, I read multiple journalists' accounts of being kidnapped, a journalist's guide to reporting while embedded with troops, and different governments' policies on negotiating with hostage takers; drafted and notarized a will; went to graduate school partly for language courses and travel vaccinations; and arranged for insurance policies that specified compensation for losing a square inch of skull, a thumb, an eye, and so on, repatriation of remains,

---

8. For complicated reasons, at this point in my life I was willing to listen to the requirements of the work I was doing, but not to God.

and a number of other contingencies, on which I spent my savings from a year of work. I applied for and received my visa and purchased plane tickets to Kabul. A series of contacts passed me on to a *Washington Post* reporter who, possibly out of pity and the hope of averting disaster, offered me a room in the *Post*'s rented house in Kabul and a connection to a fixer. I did all these things while numb with fear. I told almost no one what I was doing, apart from my family, because it was impossible to explain.

The day before I flew out, I read an essay in the *New York Times* by a writer who set her novel in China, where she had never been. She declared that she did not have to go to China to write about it, because she owned an antique Chinese teacup and an Oriental carpet, and could imagine the country in sufficient detail from owning these things.

I went.

Physiologically, courage has never gotten easier. Nine years after that research trip, and two years after the resultant novel was published, I found myself once again lying awake night after night, horrified by the story that I saw I would have to write. If published, it was likely to cost me both my good name and my career as a writer, bring a thousand modern-day witchfinders down upon my head, cause friends to denounce me in public, and lead to publishers' panicked withdrawals of my books from publication. But it was precisely because such extreme punishment for writing a short story was possible in the United States in the twenty-first century that the story had to be written. I felt the same overwhelming nausea and dread as I had before, the same anger at the obligation, the same reluctance to obey.

In George MacDonald's *The Golden Key*, there is a point where the girl named Tangle cannot go farther without leaping headfirst into darkness:

The Old Man of the Earth stooped over the floor of the cave, raised a huge stone from it, and left it leaning. It disclosed a great hole that went plumb-down.

"That is the way," he said.

"But there are no stairs."

"You must throw yourself in. There is no other way."

She turned and looked him full in the face — stood so for a whole minute, as she thought: it was a whole year — then threw herself headlong into the hole.[9]

The comfort of the passage, such as it is, lies in its depiction of such moments, such tests, as a normal part of one's progress through life. Tangle also takes time to gather the courage needed, and we are reminded that this too is permitted.

Eight months later, I had completed the story.

---

9. George MacDonald, *The Golden Key* (Grand Rapids, MI: Eerdmans Books for Young Readers, 2016), 95.

The contents of that story would have been considered unremarkable and inoffensive, if implausible, only a decade prior. And yet, as the result of a Puritan frenzy last seen in the McCarthy era, and before that in Anthony Comstock's time, fomented in every case by wealthy and duplicitous men, I cannot say what will happen to me by the time this book is published, if it is released at all.

I know the eventual cost is everything, which is true whether one obeys the call or not. Nobody takes anything out of this world, and no one lives forever. But God has had mercy on me thus far, and I have never paid in full what I expected to pay.

That said, there is a cost to cowardice as well. It is the persistent and inescapable awareness of one's failure to act, to answer the summons, to become more perfectly oneself. If that cost is set beside the cost of courage, the decision seems less staggering, even reasonable. I have learned to move toward courage, however sickening the sensations, because no matter how unhappy I am about whatever I must pay, I do not regret it afterward, whereas I regret my failures to act with courage and integrity for years thereafter. In the latter case I am disappointed with myself, and I am also aware of God's gentle disappointment in me. It took me decades of failing in this way to learn to balance my accounting of the costs. But even those failures were not wasted.

The Greek word for sin, *hamartia*, means in its most literal sense "missing the mark." It is natural to expect a novice archer is to miss, over and over, while training to hit the target. Someone walking onto an archery range for the first time has not yet developed the inner sense of accuracy, of rightness in the aim, or the steady arm and form required to shoot consistently. These things come with practice and attention. It is unreasonable to demand instant perfection in marksmanship, but reasonable to expect gradual improvement over time. The same is true of courage. For Rollo May, people become more fully human through the series of small, courageous decisions that they make and commit to day after day.[10] If we seek to tell the truth in unimportant matters, whether that is expressing our appreciation for a widely mocked film, admitting to ourselves the envy or malice behind our behavior, or setting down in watercolors and ink the lines, curves, shades, and shapes that we see, then we are practicing and preparing for the moment when a greater courage and a harder thing will be asked of us. When that time arrives, an archer who has nocked, drawn, and loosed a thousand arrows is more likely to send an arrow home to the mark than an archer who has shot only thrice.

In addition to this daily practice of courage, we are also able to receive it by grace from God. Those who believe, and even those who do not, can ask God to provide us with what we lack, whether that is courage, wisdom, love,

---

10. May, *The Courage to Create*, 13.

discernment, patience, endurance, or faith. As a loving father gives his children what is required for the day, He will give us what is good for us. We can also ask Christ to bear on our behalf our fears, anxieties, grief, pain, anger, and hate. The subjective experience rarely involves the immediate removal of my fears, but when my soul reaches the breaking point, it does not break. I have also found it helpful to pray, aware of my own inadequacy, "God, I cannot love so-and-so right now. Please love this person for me." Or: "God, I am afraid, but do not let me fail you."

Other, better Christians might aspire to the courage of Isaiah, who said to God, "Here I am! Send me" (Isa. 6:8), or of Mary, who said to the Lord, "Let it be to me according to your word" (Luke 1:38). These examples are too high for me. In contrast to Isaiah, I have lain awake praying, in vain, "Here I am, Lord—please don't send me. Send anyone else." In contrast to Mary, I have told God, "You can't be serious." What I ask for instead is the faith and courage of Ananias. When ordered by God to lay his hands upon a vicious man, Saul of Tarsus, who was violently persecuting the church, Ananias protested, presenting all the reasons why this was a terrible idea (Acts 9). I have the same reflexive response to God when He makes arduous requests of me, the same impulse to produce a slide deck titled Why Your Idea Sucks, O Lord. Usually I conclude my presentation by saying, "This is crazy. Who do you think you are—God?"

God responded to Ananias by insisting that he go and put his hands on Saul, because the result would be worthwhile. I imagine that Ananias flung up his hands and said, "Sure, whatever, it's my funeral." Trembling and terrified, he did what God asked of him. The outcome of that one act of courage was the conversion of Saul, better known as Paul, whose definition of love (1 Cor. 13:4–8) would reverberate through the next two thousand years.

It is the reluctant courage and argumentative obedience of Ananias that I hope for, and ask God to give me, and have received. With that courage, I say not "Amen," as a more perfect Christian would do, but "Fine. We'll do it Your way. It'll go badly—just watch."

Things have never gone as badly as I expect.

It is of course always better to be joyful and do good (Eccles. 3:12) and to obey God promptly and without hesitation, as Mary and Isaiah did. Someday I may reach that standard of conduct. But in Matthew 21:28–31, Jesus reminds his listeners that a surly son who first refuses to do the work his father assigns, then goes and does it, has still carried out his father's will. The imperfect, the grumpy, and the frightened have their portion to contribute, so long as they do the work that is theirs.

The problem of acquiring courage is an acute one for writers, because a book is the labor of years, and a book written without courage does not last. The slightest familiarity with actuarial tables tells me I have only so many years to live, and therefore only so many books to write, perhaps even fewer than I might hope for. If every one of those books is to become what it should, burning without consuming, stirring the soul to be strong, I myself must be brave and steadfast, which I am not. Day by day, I have to pray for the courage to finish the course in as flying a manner as I began. I have to trust that God will give me what I need to complete the task at hand, whether book or life, if I but ask. I do these things in doubt, in fear, in trembling, in darkness, sometimes in bitterness and despair. But I do them.

Three months before her death, Sophie Scholl wrote to her fiancé, Fritz Hartnagel, about her uncertainty, fear, mistrust, and exhaustion. She could no longer sense the presence of God when she prayed or when she spoke His name. Nevertheless, she said, she continued to pray: "I shall cling to the rope God has thrown me in Jesus Christ, even if my numb hands can no longer feel it."[11] She clung. The rope held.

Out of that darkness blazed a blinding light.

---

11. Letters from November 7 and 18, 1942. Sophie and Hans Scholl, *At the Heart of the White Rose: Letters and Diaries of Hans and Sophie Scholl*, edited by Inge Jens (Walden, NY: Plough Publishing House), 281–283.

Chapter Seven

SOLITUDE

ONE OF THE GRANDEST LIES OF THE TWENTY-FIRST century is the promise that constant connectivity will eliminate loneliness from human life. We are offered virality, followers, and fame in exchange for our privacy and solitude. This is a Faustian bargain for the artist. Relinquishing privacy and solitude, which closely touch the source of art, risks the loss of one's artistic capabilities. In the strip-mining of a mountain or the clearcutting of a forest, a complex, interrelated system is torn to pieces for short-term profit. Root-tips and mycelia are exposed, shelter and sustenance destroyed, the soil eroded, nutrients

washed away. Not much grows in those places afterward, and what does regrow is different. A similar process
obtains with the soul.

Haste to gain public approval or praise can prevent artists and art from achieving their full stature. "Being an
artist means: not numbering and counting, but ripening
like a tree, which doesn't force its sap," Rilke writes in
his *Letters to a Young Poet*. To an artist or a tree, "a year
doesn't matter, and ten years are nothing."[1] Like a tree,
the creative self sips water from secret places and draws
nourishment from a slow layering, decaying, and mix-
ing of matter. Given time, privacy, darkness, moisture,
and the invisible nibbling of tiny forms of life, small soft
mosses and lichens can crumble stone, shelf fungi topple
a fifty-foot tree, or a sapling split a boulder in two. For the
artist who has a sufficiency of time and privacy, very little
is unachievable.

Those same processes, that eating, drinking, and enrich-
ing of the creative self, deepen both the artist and his art,
not in a day but a decade. Depth stabilizes and strengthens
us.[2] With it, we can drink from aquifers in a drought and
stand fast in a storm. Without it, we are "carried about by
every wind of doctrine, by human cunning, by craftiness in

---

1. Rainer Maria Rilke, *Letters to a Young Poet*, trans. Stephen Mitchell (New
York: Vintage Books, 1986), 24.
2. See Hannah Arendt, *Responsibility and Judgment* (New York: Schocken
Books, 2003), 95.

deceitful schemes" (Eph. 4:14). This hidden dimension that I am speaking of has nothing to do with the approval of others, with the roar of the crowd, or with the endless production of flat, false images. It is as private and individual as courage, in that no one can deepen the life of another, although, like courage, the revealing of one person's depths can inspire others to seek the same.

Long periods of solitude and quiet are essential to the development of an artist, not only for creating art, but also for absorbing and digesting every kind of experience, investigating one's tastes and inclinations and the reasons for their existence, and listening for the quiet voice within that knows better than we know. The modern world provides scant opportunity for these contemplative practices, since they do not result in purchases, profit, or gross domestic product, but they are as necessary for artists in the present as they were in medieval times. The artist who cannot find or fight for that solitude, privacy, and quiet, if only within herself, will be stunted and stunned.

The obverse of solitude is loneliness. The fear of loneliness can drive people into self-destructive marriages, unhappy friendships, and financial scams. But loneliness is no more escapable than one's shadow. That the fundamental human condition is one of aloneness has been known for thousands of years.[3] "The Solitude of Self," Elizabeth

---

3. See Psalm 25:16, Numbers 11:17, 1 Kings 14:13, and Proverbs 9:12.

Cady Stanton's 1892 retirement speech, gives a clear-eyed account of the situation:

> Alike amid the greatest triumphs and darkest tragedies of life, we walk alone. On the divine heights of human attainment, eulogized and worshipped as a hero or saint, we stand alone. In ignorance, poverty and vice, as a pauper or criminal, alone we starve or steal....In hours like these we realize the awful solitude of individual life, its pains, its penalties, its responsibilities.[4]

The specific context of Stanton's speech was an ongoing fight for the education and enfranchisement of women in the United States. The Civil War had created a large cohort of widows and unmarried women who had to support themselves without expectation of marriage, and education offered one path to self-sufficiency.[5] Like every other human being, in extremity, women are ultimately alone, each one responsible for herself and her decisions.

---

4. Elizabeth Cady Stanton, "The Solitude of Self," in *The Women's Column* 5, no. 4 (January 23, 1892): 2–3. It might have been inspired by these lines in Elizabeth Barrett Browning's *Aurora Leigh* (1856), book 2, ll. 436–439:
    You forget too much
    That every creature, female as the male,
    Stands single in responsible act and thought
    As also in birth and death.
5. Rosalind Rosenberg, "The Limits of Access: The History of Coeducation in America," in *Women and Higher Education*, edited by John Mack Faragher and Florence Howe (New York: W. W. Norton, 1988), 109–111.

Therefore, Stanton argued, women ought to be supported and encouraged in their education and granted the rights and standing of full citizens. But her observations apply more generally. Only by accepting the lonely, solitary responsibility for one's life and one's choices, although those choices may sometimes be restricted, does one enter into maturity.

When we come to accept this aloneness, we find unexpected company, "the company of ourselves," as Hannah Arendt puts it. For Arendt, the most unbearable loneliness is nothing more and nothing less than "being deserted by oneself" after betraying the self.[6] This desolation can arise in the middle of a crowd, or in a marriage. When we become aware of this self that witnesses, to which we are bound for a lifetime, and the corresponding need to be able to live with ourselves, we may make tougher and more courageous decisions. Further, being a compassionate, loyal, and honest friend to oneself diminishes the suffering in isolation, ostracization, bereavement, or separation. It also teaches us to be compassionate, loyal, and honest in our other friendships.

At times we may believe that we are alone or unique in our suffering. This is in many cases an illusion. God often exposes the lie by placing us near someone undergoing similar trials, so that we can encourage each other. When we

---

6. Arendt, *Responsibility and Judgment*, 96.

think ourselves alone, we can pray for that kind of proximity. We also find companionship in books, art, and music with artists and saints from every era. The artist's pain, Baldwin says, is what connects him to other people's pain, and by describing what it is like to suffer, the artist can relieve both his own pain and others'.[7] Remember that Christ upon the cross, rejected by the world and abandoned by the Father, quoted the Psalms. And the veil was torn.

Our misapprehension of the roots of loneliness is sickening our society. The United States is experiencing an epidemic of loneliness that closely tracks the spread of smartphones and social media.[8] In 1967, referring to the spread of television, Guy Debord described contemporary life as being a "society of the spectacle," controlled by mass media, mass marketing, and politics, where manufactured images and scripted performances were mistaken for representations of reality. A society mesmerized by spectacle, that is, by performances and images, believes that "Everything that appears is good; whatever is good will appear."[9] In such a society, anything with depth,

---

7. Baldwin, "The Artist's Struggle for Integrity," in *The Cross of Redemption*, 53.

8. See, among many other studies on this subject, Jean M. Twenge et al., "Worldwide Increases in Adolescent Loneliness," *Journal of Adolescence* 93 (2021): 257–269, https://doi.org/10.1016/j.adolescence.2021.06.006. The effect may be global, as Twenge et al. found an increase in adolescent loneliness after 2012 in thirty-six of thirty-seven countries.

9. Thesis 12 in Guy Debord, *The Society of the Spectacle*, trans. Donald Nicholson-Smith (New York: Zone Books, 2017), 15.

anything that resists appearing, might as well not exist. But no one becomes wiser, more brilliantly alive, or more fully human through the production and consumption of these images. Nor do images provide lasting satisfaction or meaning. The consumer of images does not dream and pursue his own dreams but is reduced to an economic function in the image-producing industry. For this reason the spectacle, like any other ideology, results in the "impoverishment, enslavement and negation of real life."[10]

Echoing Debord, in his 1994 book *The Gutenberg Elegies*, Sven Birkerts looked at the spread of electronic media and communication and predicted a future in which human beings are so thoroughly woven into networks, and so bombarded with information, that they lose their privacy, depth, capacity for wisdom, and the ability to become richly and uniquely themselves.[11] Three decades on, we live in the future Birkerts feared, where everyone with an internet or mobile connection is invited and even pressured to join a mass surveillance regime. Each of us is urged to publish our private thoughts and personal information, or a simulacrum thereof, for the judgment, titillation, and entertainment of cruel and foolish strangers we would not ordinarily meet. Even those who decline to participate are subtly affected by the existence

10. Thesis 215 in Debord, *The Society of the Spectacle*, 151.
11. Sven Birkerts, *The Gutenberg Elegies: The Fate of Reading in an Electronic Age* (New York: Faber and Faber, 2006), 130–131.

of that vast impenetrable network. As long as others are willing to credit its claims and bow to its demands, no one is free from that panopticon. It does not matter that some accounts have been unmasked as foreign intelligence agents playacting at being American from offices in Moscow, or that many are con men acting various roles. In practice, most people have trouble identifying the provocateurs in the middle of a mob, or imposters in a network of millions. Almost no one remembers that "hypocrite" derives from the Greek word for a stage actor.

Because I have caught and eaten many trout and a few salmon, I know well how nets catch, hold, and control. Online networks that deliberately manipulate the brain's secretion of dopamine not only catch and hold our attention but rewire our neural pathways, without our being conscious of the alteration. On Twitter and analogous sites, C. Thi Nguyen notes, users receive constant updates on engagement metrics. Over time, they are trained to behave in ways that improve those metrics, and not in ways that honor their values, relationships, or humanity, which are not measurable or monetizable. The individual who subjects her own good judgment to the comments and upvotes of an artificial crowd has abdicated the responsibility to know and act according to her own values, to think independently, and to "test everything" and "hold fast what is good" (1 Thess. 5:21). As Nguyen puts it, "Being guided by an aggregate measure of the audience's approval is a far cry from being guided by one's own internal sense of value."[12] This substitution of what is popular, of what performs well, for one's personal compass, the conscience and the quiet voice within, is an immeasurable loss. Real and vital creativity disappears, replaced by a pale and watery imitation. Courage withers on the vine.[13]

I have heard writer after writer express anxiety or nervously joke about the prospect of being targeted by online mobs, with the same high strain in the voice I have heard in authoritarian countries where writers and journalists are imprisoned for their words. Although our right of expression is constitutionally protected, social-media mobbing and fabricated outrage can result in job loss, withdrawn books, canceled contracts and events, death threats, rape threats, bomb threats, stalking, and assault, particularly when the target is female. This environment of pervasive threat is not conducive to good literature, good art, or good conversation. Rather, it promotes fawning, cringing, fighting, backstabbing, moral grandstanding,

---

12. C. Thi Nguyen, "How Twitter Gamifies Communication," in *Applied Epistemology*, edited by Jennifer Lackey (Oxford: Oxford University Press, 2021), 416.

13. It has become common to see and hear the question "What do we think of so-and-so or such-and-such?" I know of no starker sign of the bankruptcy of the intellect. Unwilling to think for herself or to form her own opinion and taste, the asker delegates all cognitive and aesthetic responsibilities to the crowd. What is spewed forth later as the asker's supposed opinion is nothing but a copy of popular and flattering ideas.

scapegoating, informing on others, and every form of cowardice and cruelty.

That said, the past decade of mob rule is nothing but the most recent manifestation of an old phenomenon. Every now and then, Baldwin says, America transforms into "the grimmest of popularity contests," obsessed with public approval, resulting in a "quite insane system of penalties and rewards." The artist only survives, Baldwin says, by leaving America for a time, so that he can learn to accept his own, individual view of the world and thereby become himself, which cannot happen amid gladiatorial battles for popularity and acclaim.[14] The process of *becoming oneself* that Baldwin writes about has nothing to do with plastic surgery, clothing purchases, or the enforced control of other people's words and perceptions. It is unrelated to image curation and reputation management. It has everything to do with putting down roots, establishing depth, and breaking through the boulders buried in the self. These are long and private labors that no one else can see, but without them we are blown about by the weather of the world.

Sooner or later, a storm comes. Then, depending on whether we have poured our time and energy into striking roots or have spent them on shallow and superficial matters, we shall either withstand its force or fall.

---

14. Baldwin, "The New Lost Generation," in *The Price of the Ticket*, 320.

No one becomes a true artist, writing and speaking life and reality, without undergoing an exile of the kind Baldwin describes, discovering aloneness, and accepting it.[15] Such artists have always been few, since the exile is lifelong and difficult, but their numbers at present seem exceptionally thin. Meanwhile, we drown in a proliferation of ersatz artists, who slot smoothly into the machinery of spectacle and stamp out lifeless nothings. The prospect is admittedly discouraging.

At the same time, there is no reason to believe that the insane system described by Baldwin, Debord, Birkerts, and Nguyen is permanent or indestructible. It will collapse if enough people are willing to bear responsibility for themselves and to think rather than conform, consume, and indulge. While this would revive a decadent and decaying society, thinking and bearing responsibility are not altruistic acts. They involve nothing less than the reclamation of one's life, independence, and humanity. And this process of becoming takes solitude and privacy.

---

15. Also see Hebrews 11:13.

III

Chapter Eight

GOD THE COLLABORATOR

G OD, WHAT AND WHEN AND HOW DO YOU WANT ME
to write?

God, help me.

With these invocations I greet the blank page. Nor am I the only artist to do so. Jerome Hines, sitting down to write an opera, prayed, "God, write this music for me. Of myself I cannot."[1] Flannery O'Connor wrote in her prayer journal: "Dear God please help me to be an artist, please

---

1. Jerome Hines, *This Is My Story, This Is My Song* (Westwood, NJ: Fleming H. Revell Company, 1968), 47.

let it lead to You."[2] Bach sometimes wrote "J. J.," for *Jesu Juva*, "Help, Jesus," at the top of his manuscripts, and "S. D. Gl.," for *Soli Deo Gloria*, "Glory to God alone," at the end.[3] Haydn inscribed *Laus deo*, "Praise God," at the end of every manuscript. He described the composition of *The Creation* to Stendhal in this way: "Before sitting down to the piano, I would quietly and confidently pray to God to grant me the talent that was needed to praise Him worthily."[4] Dvořák, similarly, to his publisher Simrock: "I shall simply do what God tells me to do, that will certainly be the best thing."[5] Everyone who writes and speaks in this way is echoing the words of Brother Lawrence, who said: "Lord, I cannot do this unless Thou enablest me."[6]

2. Entry dated April 14, 1947. Flannery O'Connor, *A Prayer Journal* (New York: Farrar, Straus and Giroux, 2013), 29.
3. Friedrich Blume, *Two Centuries of Bach: An Account of Changing Tastes* (London: Oxford University Press, 1950), 14; Albert Schweitzer, *J. S. Bach* (New York: Dover Publications, 1911), 284. Both citations found through Patrick Kavanaugh's *The Spiritual Lives of the Composers*, which gives incorrect page numbers for Schweitzer. All three authors have stated the case more strongly than I have here. Skimming a handful of digitized manuscripts, these notations appear somewhat rare: BWV 191 has "J.J." and "Gloria Patri," BWV 651 and 1052 have "J.J.," and BWV 1058 has "S.D.Gl."
4. Henri Beyle (Stendhal), *Haydn, Mozart, and Metastasio* (New York: Grossman, 1972), 149–150. Cited in Kavanaugh, *The Spiritual Lives of the Composers*, 41.
5. Neil Butterworth, *Dvořák, His Life and Times* (Kent: Midas, 1980), 45. Partially quoted in Kavanaugh, *The Spiritual Lives of the Composers*, 154, with wrong page number.
6. Brother Lawrence, *The Practice of the Presence of God* (New York: Fleming H. Revell, 1895), 17.

In this day and age, it may seem anachronistic to aspire to eternal works, or to ask for help from God with a painting or a poem. But we do not have any chance of accomplishing the first without the second. This used to be better known.

To apprentice oneself to a master artist, past or present, single or several, is the beginner's first step toward excellence. Because I know no better artist than the first Creator, the first Artist, the Author and Perfector, who dreamed and then exploded nothingness into everything, it is at the door to His workshop that I am presently knocking. Apprentices are instructed, but also restricted, disciplined, and assigned both scutwork and challenges. With the proper teacher, however, who is dedicated to the apprentice's growth, there is steady improvement, industry, and delight. Every artist who chooses to labor in this way, in collaboration with the Creator, finds another, stronger hand upon his own and another, higher vision regulating his. The work that results will exceed his natural abilities.[7] Such artists—including Bach, Brahms, Puccini, Beethoven, Dvořák, Flannery O'Connor, George MacDonald, Madeleine L'Engle, and Baldwin—gratefully acknowledge the One who worked through them.

---

7. See Baldwin's speech at Kalamazoo: "To be with God is really to be involved with some enormous, overwhelming desire, and joy, and power which you cannot control, which controls you." James Baldwin, "In Search of a Majority," in *The Price of the Ticket*, 241.

In this sense, the artist's whole life is an apprenticeship to God. The same is true for Christians. The great hope of both is that whatever imperfect but faith-filled works we complete during our apprenticeship will be transformed and perfected and endure into the new creation. What we do now also serves as practice for the commissions we will receive then. MacDonald imagines the artist in the new creation as being "able to make like thee— / To light with moons, to clothe with greenery."[8] I think the artist in the new creation can expect the lapidary labors of millions of planets and asteroids, the blowing of alcohol-ink nebulae, the embroidery of auroras and galaxies.

That time is beyond my knowing. But the artist's assignment in the present is no different in nature from the work that is to come. Here and now, we are to collaborate with Him.

This does not mean what most people call *doing good*. A sister in my previous church stood up one day and said: "I've realized God does not want us to do *good*, but to do *God*." The distinction between the two is not the specific action taken but the source of the action. Either we have eaten from the tree of knowledge of good and evil, and now do what that knowledge tells us is good, or we have eaten from the tree of life, and therefore do in obedience to the Spirit's leading what we might not know to be good. Ananias did

---

8. George MacDonald, "March," in *A Book of Strife in the Form of a Diary of an Old Soul* (London: self-published, 1880), 49.

not do good, as he saw it, in healing a persecutor of the church, but he did God's will, and the world was changed. It was Saul of Tarsus, the destroyer, who did what seemed righteous and lawful in his own eyes. That type of goodness, or more accurately self-righteousness, comes from the self and not from God. The same can be said of the Pharisees who dragged a woman to Jesus and asked permission to stone her, since she had broken the law. These men, doing what they considered correct, justified by doctrine and each other, missed what was in the heart of God.

Not all who claim to be artists are the genuine article, and not all who say "Lord, Lord" will be recognized by God (Matt. 7:21). But the difference between the true artist and the not-yet-true artist, or the empty semblance of a Christian and the real servant of God, is at once as vast, as consequential, and as minuscule as the difference between Saul on the road to Damascus and the Saul who wrote "Love is patient, love is kind." It is nothing more and nothing less than time, revelation, and a series of decisions that lead to the living God becoming the source of our thoughts, words, actions, life, and art. Artists do not differ from Christians in this regard. "Poets and other artists," Raïssa Maritain writes, "the great inventors and the saints, all draw on the same divine source.... They are all of them imitators of God."[9]

---

9. Raïssa Maritain, *Poetry and Mysticism* (Wiseblood Books, 2022), 18.

To have God as our source, we must be in an intimate and immediate relationship with Him. It is only possible to learn what He wants by asking Him directly. The so-called Christian artist who fails to do so, who writes what he thinks will please God or religious authorities, heaps up a hill of words that in spite of their piety is lacking in Christ and thus lacking in life. L'Engle called such work *pornographic*, while Flannery O'Connor's term for it was *propaganda*.[10] Such work takes the name of God in vain. It cheapens what many have lived and died for and teaches a falsehood in place of the truth.

Through the joint disciplines of prayer and meditation we may approach and converse with God. By prayer I mean addressing, petitioning, and thanking God; calling for His help; asking how we have gone against His will; confessing and repenting of the ways we have done so; and requesting His forgiveness and blessing.[11] By meditation, or contemplation, I mean a posture of deep attentiveness, of careful listening for His response. The two practices are continuous with each other, and insofar as I remember to do them, continuous with my living and my writing as well. "The time of business does not with me differ

---

10. L'Engle, *The Rock That Is Higher*, 188; letter to Father J. H. McCown dated May 9, 1956, in Flannery O'Connor, *The Habit of Being*, edited by Sally Fitzgerald (New York: Farrar, Straus, and Giroux, 1979), 157.

11. Jeanne Guyon's *Experiencing the Depths of Jesus Christ* (Jacksonville, FL: Seedsowers Publishing, 1975) and John Eldredge's *Moving Mountains* (Nashville: Thomas Nelson, 2016) were exceptionally helpful to me.

from the time of prayer," Brother Lawrence said,[12] which suggests what is meant by the command to "pray without ceasing" (1 Thess. 5:17). While writing, driving, or conversing with others, my prayer is that what I say or write or do might be according to His will and not my own.

As I was writing and rewriting my first novel, I had many conversations and several heated arguments with God. The most intimate collaboration was when I invited Him to edit the fourth draft, figuring that if He was Author and Perfector, as He said, He would make an excellent Editor as well. Over a day and a night, I prayed over every paragraph, asking God if He wanted any changes, making those changes, then asking again. I did not move to the next paragraph until I had peace to do so. When I finished praying, at around four or five in the morning, the manuscript was essentially complete, though not yet perfect, and ready to be sent to agents.

"Every single one of us, without exception, is called to co-create with God," L'Engle writes.[13] That calling is a sweet and an urgent one. It is possible to refuse the cutting and shaping that make the artist an instrument in the hand of God. If the reed that should have been cut, carved, and blown upon, turning God's breath to music, stays in place and avoids the knife, it withers and sinks silently back into the marsh. The silver that should have

---

12. Brother Lawrence, *The Practice of the Presence of God*, 30.
13. Madeleine L'Engle, *And It Was Good* (New York: Convergent, 2017), 7.

been smelted, rolled, and assembled with keys and valves to play hymns of praise may remain tongueless and hidden in gangue. One can also be well fashioned and refuse to play. Love goes where it is invited and welcomed. It does not force a way, does not break down doors, does not coerce. Because love is a choice, it requires free will and does not exist where there is no possibility of refusal. That we might love and collaborate with the One who created us is His longing and hope, and our glory, if we do; that we frequently refuse the invitation is attested to by all the horrors in history.

I am speaking here of faith and not of religion. When religion lacks faith, which is often the case, it is a loveless, lifeless ossuary. What has called itself the Church across the ages has tortured and killed more Christians than the Romans ever did. Many who call themselves Christians attach the name of God to idols bearing little resemblance to Him, or make God in their own image and worship themselves by proxy.[14] The opposite process is asked of us. We are meant to become more and more conformed to God's life and image, ever clearer and more transparent, until the rest of the world sees not our selves but the unwavering light that shines out of us. Wherever I have

---

14. Two symptoms are strongly indicative: a total lack of humor and a vicious pleasure in condemning women for being women. These often go together.

seen that light, in however many countries, in however many faces, I know the source is one.

There is no obligation to be perfect, because only One has ever been perfect. We are asked to be ready and willing; that is all. God, being our Perfector, will supply what we lack. As the master artist provides apprentices with pigments, canvas, and tools, He will give us what is needed to carry out His work. Often we do not understand the larger import of our tasks before we carry them out. Léon Bloy pictures the world as infinite and interconnected through time and space, where if someone begrudgingly gives a penny to a poor man, the coin pierces the man's hand, falls, pierces the earth, bores through suns, crosses the firmament, and compromises the universe, while an act of true charity likewise reverberates backwards and forwards through history.[15] Limited by our coarse senses, we seldom perceive any but the most violent of these creation-spanning tremors. I have to trust that God attends to them, and that the single stroke of paint I am asked to lay down with my life will become part of a joyful and ordered whole. This is not easy to do. When I am adrift, I cling to Isaiah 55:8–9, which reminds us that

---

15. "Si'l donne de mauvais coeur un sou à un pauvre, ce sou perce la main du pauvre, tombe, perce la terre, troue les soleils, traverse le firmament et compromet l'univers." Léon Bloy, *Le Désespéré* (Paris: Nouvelle Librairie A. Soirat, 1887), 128. I am indebted to Raïssa Maritain's *Poetry and Mysticism* (Menomonee Falls, WI: Wiseblood Books, 2022), 29, for drawing my attention to the passage.

God's ways are not our ways, and that His thoughts are of a higher order than ours. At other times, when I think I have finally understood Him, I am promptly turned tail over teakettle and discover once again that He is again deeper than oceanic trenches and as far beyond my kenning as the faintest star.

One thing I do know. Because God is the master artist and our Creator, in whose image we are made, whose imagination fashioned our own imaginations,[16] when we are called to create, it is after His pattern, in love. The present conversation about ethics in art and writing, focusing on identities both synthetic and situational, the giving and taking of offense, and a naked competition for power, attention, and the appearance of virtue, misses this point entirely. God created out of love and delighted in life, and when He looked upon His work, He pronounced it good. He has never created in contempt, disgust, or hatred. We are meant to follow His example. By this I mean that the author is responsible for loving every character she creates, however unlovable their actions and thoughts. The reader does not have to love the most detestable characters, the other characters do not have to love them, but the author must. Love does not mean giving them smooth and untroubled lives or approving of what they do. Nor does it

---

16. "The imagination of man is made in the imagination of God." George MacDonald, "The Imagination: Its Functions and Its Culture" in *A Dish of Orts* (London: Samson Low, Marston & Company, 1895), 3.

mean scheduling their punishment and destruction before the end of the book. It does mean granting them freedom and life, inasmuch as characters in a book can be free and alive. It means hoping for and desiring their good, and imagining a beautiful part and place for them in the whole, however unlikely the prospect of their reaching it.

If a novel is to say something true about what it means to be human, which is to say, free and alive even in the most crushing circumstances,[17] then the characters must have freedom and life as well. They must be capable of surprising the author, possessing a willfulness that forces the story out of its expected path. They should not be limp dolls dragged here and there, posed and made to ventriloquize the author's favorite political slogans.[18] Their dialogue should be in their individual voices and not the author's, they should speak out of their accumulated experiences, and their words should be fresh and original, because human beings think and speak differently from one another.[19]

17. This is the freedom that Viktor Frankl found in a concentration camp, that Kayla Mueller meant when she wrote "I have been shown in darkness, light + have learned that even in prison, one can be free." "Kayla Mueller's Letter to Her Family," *New York Times*, February 10, 2015, https://nyti.ms/3Yid32w.
18. See Jacques Maritain, *Creative Intuition*, 125–126; Frederick Buechner, "Two Narrow Words," in *Secrets in the Dark: A Life in Sermons* (New York: HarperCollins, 2006), 166.
19. This is less true when human beings are subjugated by an authoritarian system. Even in that extremity, however, there are those who, like Sophie and Hans Scholl, like Viktor Frankl, like Madame Guyon, will keep "the joy, the freedom of the mind."

Extensive revisions are usually required for characters to be realized in this way, but just as God gave us independence, creativity, and the capacity for love, the author should strive to give these things to her characters. When we succeed, when we come to love the least beloved part of our creation and free all of our characters to be as cooperative or rebellious as they choose, we have learned something about the mind and heart of the One who created us.

This freedom on the part of the characters does not imply chaos at the formal level of the book. God, considering the span of eternity, weaves even the worst snarls into His design. The Creator remains responsible for working all things together to good (Rom. 8:28), for making all things beautiful in their time (Eccles. 3:11), for transforming the most misdirected actions, that everything may be gathered up and reordered into a life-affirming whole. In the same way, the author's unifying vision must be too high and clear for her characters' freedom to confound. Likewise, she bears the responsibility of working all things together for good, of suffusing even the most brutal moments with beauty and significance. "The truest joy of art...is to force recalcitrant matter into the beauty and meaning God gives it," Sister Wendy Beckett wrote in a letter in 1976.[20] For all our smallness and imperfection, when we construct and reconstruct a novel until every

---

20. Letter dated September 9, 1976. Sister Wendy Beckett, *Spiritual Letters* (Maryknoll, NY: Orbis Books, 2013), 50.

moment rings with meaning and merges with the whole, we are working in the same way that God is working, and we participate in His satisfaction and joy.

Too much art these days is created not out of love but contempt, though it may be wrapped in spun sugar to hide the bitterness. I have put down book after book where the writer displays contempt for certain characters, contempt for the reader, contempt for the craft and the calling. Cookie-cutter dialogue in books and films, or fussy lectures conforming to whatever Puritan code is fashionable today,[21] are clear signs that one is among puppets and marionettes, and not anything that can move and speak for itself. The word *cliché* derives from the French *clicher*, "to click," and originally referred to the plate known as a stereotype that falls with a click upon page after page, stamping out reproductions of a text. Books that indulge in clichés are written for clicks, cliques, and claques. They offer only tired impressions duplicated from elsewhere. Such books do not say anything real or revelatory about what it is to be human, to love, to bear responsibility, to suffer, to change. They confirm the poverty of imagination, the defeat of creativity, and the spreading inability to see other people as richly and fully human in the present age.

---

21. This is distinct from historically appropriate lectures exhibiting whatever form of Puritanism applies to the period of the book. One grows naturally from the substrate of the story, while the other is imposed from the book's exterior.

Put more plainly, any creator is ultimately responsible to her creation. If she cannot love and care for the people and the world that she invents, if she does not invest them with her own aliveness, if she does not treat language and craft with respect, it would be better if she did not create. Many other roads remain open to her: politics, mathematics, or chemistry, for example. The world does not need more novels written with indifference, greed, or contempt; it is surfeited with them already.

If, however, we choose to be apprenticed to God the Artist, learning to create in our more limited ways as He creates in His, we learn how deeply we are loved, how much we are forgiven, how willing He is to guide and support us, if we ask. If we create in collaboration with Him, listening for His direction and correction, He will make what we create together beautiful and useful, in ways we cannot guess at, and may not live to see. If we allow Him to coauthor our lives, then He will make us, flawed as we are, beautiful and useful as well.

Why not think of God, Rilke wrote to a doubting young man, as the "ultimate fruit of the tree whose leaves we all are?"[22] Live in hope of that coming, Rilke suggested, as one looks patiently for spring and its unfolding. Two hundred years prior, Brother Lawrence was moved to faith at the age of eighteen by the sight of a tree in winter and

22. Rainer Maria Rilke, *Letters to a Young Poet*, trans. Stephen Mitchell (New York: Vintage Books, 1986), 61.

thoughts of its resurrection in spring, a faith that led him to collaborate with God in even the most menial tasks. However transitory the leaves that unfurl in spring, fall in autumn, and return as nutrients to the root, they point to and grow out of a stronger, higher life that persists through winter into spring, slowly gathering itself toward fruitfulness. Artist or Christian, when we eat and drink of the divine life that reconfigures our own, when we sink our own roots through soil and stone, we become so many trees beside that river that proceeds from the throne of God, withstanding drought, fire, and frost, each year putting forth the soft green signs of resurrection.

"And the leaves of the tree are for the healing of the nations" (Rev. 22:2 NIV).

Chapter Nine

SO GREAT A CLOUD
OF WITNESSES

Although in the end we are alone with God, alone answerable for our lives and decisions, alone choosing to say either "Thy will be done" or "My will be done," we are not without models, comforters, and teachers. I sometimes imagine a library where threads fine as spider silk stretch from book to book, showing how one was influenced by another, or how a friendship, or one author's admiration for another, leaves traces upon those writers' books. The threads would drift so thickly in parts that one

189

could scarcely find a way between them. To take one particular example, perhaps a thousand threads extend from George MacDonald's books, multiplying as they touch others.[1]

By this date, MacDonald's creative descendants might be uncountable, so I will only name the best known. Lewis Carroll not only read MacDonald's work but brought the manuscript of *Alice's Adventures Underground* to the MacDonalds, who read it to their children and advised him to publish it.[2] J. R. R. Tolkien read and loved *The Princess and the Goblin* and *The Princess and Curdie* before the age of ten, though he became resentful of MacDonald's use of allegory as an adult.[3] Mark Twain and his wife had a long friendship with the MacDonalds, and Twain asked at one point for another copy of *At the Back of the North Wind* because their children

---

1. In the other direction, MacDonald himself was strongly influenced by the Christian mystic Novalis, whose poetry he translated. Gary K. Wolfe, "George MacDonald," in *Supernatural Fiction Writers*, vol. 1, edited by E. F. Bleiler (New York: Scribner, 1985), 240.

2. See Lewis Carroll, diary entry of May 9, 1863, in Diary 4, British Library, Add MS 54343, f.75r; Stuart Dodgson Collingwood, *The Life and Letters of Lewis Carroll* (London: T. Fisher Unwin, 1898), 97; and Greville MacDonald, *George MacDonald and His Wife* (New York: Dial Press, 1924), 342.

3. Humphrey Carpenter, *J. R. R. Tolkien: A Biography* (New York: Houghton Mifflin Harcourt, 2000), 30; Jason Fisher, "Reluctantly Inspired: George MacDonald and J. R. R. Tolkien," *North Wind: A Journal of George MacDonald Studies* 25 (2006): 113–120, http://digitalcommons.snc.edu/northwind/vol25/iss1/8.

had loved the first copy to pieces.[4] C. S. Lewis famously called MacDonald "my master,"[5] anthologized his work, attributed his own conversion to buying a copy of *Phantastes* at a train station,[6] and cast MacDonald as Virgil to Lewis' Dante in *The Great Divorce*. Madeleine L'Engle confessed that her image of the Father was, in fact, George MacDonald, "so yes, there is a beard, but there is also deep maternal love."[7] W. H. Auden called MacDonald "one of the most remarkable writers of the nineteenth century" in an introduction to the 1954 combined edition of *Phantastes* and *Lilith*.[8] G. K. Chesterton once described *The Princess and the Goblin* as having made "a difference to my whole existence."[9]

4. Kathryn Lindskoog, "Mark Twain and George MacDonald: The Salty and the Sweet," *Mark Twain Journal* 30, no. 2 (Fall 1992): 26–32, http://www.jstor.org/stable/41641369. While I cannot prove a direct influence, Mark Twain's *Joan of Arc*, the book Twain considered the best of all his work, written after twenty-four years of correspondence with MacDonald, is easily the most MacDonaldesque of all Twain's work.
5. C. S. Lewis, "Preface," in *George MacDonald: An Anthology* (San Francisco: HarperSanFrancisco, 2001), xxxvii.
6. C. S. Lewis, *Surprised by Joy* (Boston: Houghton Mifflin Harcourt, 2012), 179–181.
7. Madeleine L'Engle, *Penguins and Golden Calves: Icons and Idols in Antarctica and Other Unexpected Places* (Colorado Springs, CO: Shaw Books, 2003), 222.
8. W. H. Auden, "Introduction," in *The Visionary Novels of George MacDonald*, edited by Anne Fremantle (New York: Noonday Press, 1954), vi.
9. G. K. Chesterton, "Introduction," in Greville MacDonald, *George MacDonald and His Wife* (New York: Dial Press, 1924), 9.

I had read MacDonald's fantastical novels before college, but it was his pair of masterworks, *The Princess and the Goblin* and *The Princess and Curdie*, that amazed me when I reread them a decade and a half later. These two books described most of what I had learned in the interim about walking with God, though the word *God* appears only once, in a meaningless interjection. They stood waiting for me at the end of my road, as warm and welcoming as ever, but subtly changed and now profound.

Chesterton, transformed by MacDonald's masterpiece, went on to write his own, *The Man Who Was Thursday*. Minister and author Frederick Buechner wrote an homage to Chesterton's novel in *Love Feast*, while Neil Gaiman borrowed the smoked spectacles from Chesterton's Dr. Bull for the Corinthian in the *Sandman* graphic novels.[10] At the end of T. S. Eliot's *Little Gidding*, following a quotation from Julian of Norwich, the fire of roses from *The Princess and Curdie* reappears in the line "And the fire and the rose are one."

These are only a few of the threads spun out of MacDonald, but they give a sense of the density and proliferation of those threads. A comparable situation exists among the Christian composers from Bach through Stravinsky and Messiaen, many of whom supported and encouraged

---

10. In another such thread, Gaiman has spoken repeatedly about how reading Lewis' *The Voyage of the Dawn Treader* and *The Lion, the Witch, and the Wardrobe* at the age of six led him to consider writing.

their contemporaries.[11] I would not be surprised to learn of parallels among the artists.

I have traced this particular genealogy, by no means the only one of its kind, because many of its leaves were working toward a single purpose. Insofar as they knew themselves to be strangers and exiles in the world, they are those for whom God prepared and promised a city (Heb. 11:13–15). But the construction of any city is a labor of generations. The stonemasons and architects of the great cathedrals, N. T. Wright reminds us, were contributing to a monumental work that would not be completed in their lifetimes, or else finishing what their grandfathers started.[12] Though dimly, I perceive that city we are invited to labor on, that Dante added graceful arches to, developing outward from the first cornerstone. Since no human work and no human being is without flaw, we need not like or admire everything that the laborers before us have left behind, nor approve of every detail of their lives, but our own art and artisanship can only be set on the stones of the city that they shaped and bequeathed to us.

The living and the dead who dressed stones for this city form that great cloud of witnesses watching us as we carry out our own work. Although I cannot see them, I think that their looks are loving, that they watch in hope of our success and rejoice in whatever sound work we do.

11. See Patrick Kavanaugh, *The Spiritual Lives of the Composers*.
12. N. T. Wright, *Surprised by Hope*, 209–210.

When the light of eternity shines through it, if only for a moment, that much of our work is joined to theirs. This is what Eliot meant when he said:

> The existing monuments form an ideal order among themselves, which is modified by the introduction of the new (the really new) work of art among them. The existing order is complete before the new work arrives; for order to persist after the supervention of novelty, the *whole* existing order must be, if ever so slightly, altered; and so the relations, proportions, values of each work of art toward the whole are readjusted.[13]

In other words, when the artist, faithfully serving Art or God, produces a high and holy work, the joyful throng parts to let the new member in, then closes around her, becoming whole once more. This is the case for artists who, being mastered, achieve mastery; it is also the case for those who enter into a new life with Christ. Neither Eliot's formulation nor mine excludes writers who were not Christian yet who created with divine life as their source. The final winnowing of hearts and works is God's.

If I look to this cloud of witnesses for encouragement, if I see how my work builds upon their foundation, if I understand that my own best efforts, by God's grace better

---

13. T. S. Eliot, "Tradition and the Individual Talent," in *The Sacred Wood*, 50.

than what I could do alone, add something to the universal effort, then I am freed from writers' ordinary heartaches and vices. The prize I pursue cannot be debated or issued by any earthly committee. It is not a foil sticker on a dust jacket or a glass or metal trophy but God's eventual transformation of my imperfect work into what is lasting and perfect in the time that is to come. There is no sense in envying other writers. Either we are working shoulder to shoulder on the same great task that was set before we were born, in which case the work progresses more quickly for having more workers, or they are chasing vanities and illusions that are none of my concern.

Although, like any human being, I will be fairly and unfairly applauded or reviled, and the same will happen to my books, I am not and have never been writing for the approval of the foolish, the cruel, the ignorant, or the vile, or even for the average person, who, as Sarah Schulman reminds us, is incapable of appreciating a genuine new work of art.[14] I write for the approval of God above all. Therefore I am also writing for the approval of those before me who would have recognized the light I am striving to let into the world, because they did the same, and know the cost; for joy and encouragement to those who travel

---

14. Schulman, *The Gentrification of the Mind*, 76; also Proust, *Within a Budding Grove*, vol. 1, 327. I wish it were otherwise. But if someone has the ability to identify a new and groundbreaking work of art, that person is no longer average.

the same road I am on; and, insofar as they and God will
it, for the growth of the rest.

It would spare many promising new writers a good deal
of suffering, and save them much time, to consider things
from the perspective of eternity. We do not, after all, have
time to waste.

Only Christ was ever meant for everyone, and even
He was rejected, slandered, mocked, spat upon, and
scourged. The artist's aim has never been popularity and
wide acceptance, that most confining and slavish of conditions, but the speaking of truth and life, in defiance
of mobs, armies, dictators, politicians, kings, commit-
tees, stakes, crosses, and every kind of religious authority. Writers and artists who seek to please malicious and
manipulative people cannot avoid being degraded, and in
the process often end up degrading others as well. "The
crowd is untruth," Søren Kierkegaard said. To follow an
uninformed crowd is to become lost; to join a panicked
crowd is to risk trampling; to howl along with a blood-
thirsty mob is to participate in murder.[15] Virginia Woolf
points out that only those women who did not respond
to scolding, admonishments, or the temptation of prizes,
who had both genius and integrity, and were able to "hold
fast to the thing as they saw it without shrinking," wrote
books that endured, while the works of those women who

---

15. "Therefore go out from their midst, and be separate from them, says the
Lord" (2 Cor. 6:17).

"altered [their] values in deference to the opinions of others" rotted like blotched apples in the middens of history.[16] Baldwin has said the same of men.[17]

For those who have read this book with incredulity, scorn, or doubt, it may be worth mentioning that the hard thing is not believing in God, though that is a passionate fixation of Christians who pride themselves on rationality and argumentation,[18] as well as of Christians who do not really know or trust in God. There is, after all, as much empirical evidence against God's existence as for it, or faith would not exist. But Matthew 7:8 and Jeremiah 29:13 promise that to anyone who knocks, the door will be opened, and that anyone who wholeheartedly seeks God will find Him. Ask the universe if God exists. Ask Him to reveal Himself to you. Then listen for the answer.

That is not the hard part. I do not think that the Creator of heaven and earth is discomposed if any person does not believe He exists. I might pity someone who says he is not sure whether or not I exist, who perhaps is struggling with reality, but I am not affected by his belief either way. If someone I love, however, tells me he doubts that I love him, that is painful. I have given much pain of this kind to God, because the hard thing is to believe that God is Love, that He loves me unfailingly, and that His will for

16. Woolf, *A Room of One's Own*, 74–75.
17. Baldwin, "The New Lost Generation," in *The Price of the Ticket*, 320.
18. Who are, to be fair, useful and necessary in certain contexts.

me is good. More than once, as water dripped through the ceiling, or as I curled up in pain, I have prayed, "Lord, do you still love me? Because it sure doesn't seem like it!" Also: "You've always taken care of me—but what about *this* time? What if this time You fail?"

He hasn't failed yet.

The way of life I am suggesting—asking God what He wants, listening carefully for the answer, then obeying—is not for the faint of heart.[19] Following Him, I bought plane tickets to Nairobi while unemployed, took an entry-level job instead of a senior-level one, spoke up in one situation and remained silent in another, put money in one man's hand and did not give to another, wrote a story I knew would destroy my reputation, and wrote a book on art and faith. I could not do these things if He had not provided the courage, faith, and grace that I lack. He has also directed my steps toward a company of writers stretching back through Baldwin, MacDonald, Chesterton, Hopkins, Rilke, Watchman Nee, and Madame Guyon to Julian of Norwich and Dante, whose words, even centuries after their deaths, comfort, console, and give courage and life. And what they say in a single voice is this: God does not promise safety, public approbation, wealth, ease, or success, and He will not spare us grief, loss, pain, and death. But God is Love, who suffered for and suffers

---

19. Whose ranks include the author.

with us, and in His hands all will be transfigured, so that one day we will see that the mortar of the shining city to which we belong holds firmer for having been mixed with our tears, and we will be glad for what was done.

That is the great mystery: how it will be done; how it is being done even now, with us and through us and for us. Humans are shortsighted, small-hearted, anxious creatures, as a rule, and it is terrifying to live by mystery and grace. This is a haunted life and a hallowed one. But I do not know any better or richer or more creative way to live.

Chapter Ten

WING, WIND, AND WORLD

Fifty years apart, two Jesuits had a near identical vision of divine light burning within the created world. Gerard Manley Hopkins wrote in 1877:

> The world is charged with the grandeur of God.
> It will flame out, like shining from shook foil...

In northern China in the 1920s, French paleontologist Pierre Teilhard de Chardin noted that every created thing, from stone to bird, if closely observed, reveals "the same reality...in their innermost being—like sunlight in the fragments of a broken mirror."[1] That unitary reality, for him, was God. Both Hopkins and Teilhard de Chardin direct us to watch nature for the "flaming out" or reflected flash, as of foil or glass, that reveals to us slantingly a shard of the glory that we cannot yet see with unveiled face. *Look*, they say. Look hard: it is there.

The day before I began writing this chapter, I paused on my walk to teach three generations of a family the shape, color, and stink of skunk cabbage; the serrated leaves of stinging nettle and its culinary value; the magenta stars of salmonberry flowers; the triply forked fronds of lady fern. Give children the smells, sounds, and tastes of the wild world, Mary Oliver pleads, that they may come to know it, and by that knowledge grow to love.[2] I had received such an inheritance early on. When I was very young, I learned from my mother the bitter deliciousness of young dandelion leaves and the species of *Sonchus* called 甜苣菜, which grows in the furrows of a planted field, as well as the species of *Nostoc* called 地皮菜, which we collected scale by soft scale from the windblown hills of her childhood home. Not long after that, I acquired a secondhand book of plants, which I matched to what was burgeoning

1. Pierre Teilhard de Chardin, *The Divine Milieu* (New York: Harper & Row, 1960), 114. Both Hopkins' poem and Teilhard de Chardin's book were published posthumously.
2. Mary Oliver, "Upstream," in *Blue Iris: Poems and Essays* (Boston: Beacon Press, 2004), 55–56.

around me, trying the green crunch of lamb's-quarters and the lemon tartness of wood sorrel.

In adulthood I picked, hulled, and fried the fiddleheads of lady fern and bracken, blanched and chopped nettles, plucked evergreen and red huckleberries, nibbled miners' lettuce, mixed mica caps into omelets. I learned the anise odor of oyster mushrooms, aniseed toadstools, and licorice fern root, along with the apricot odor of chanterelles. I know their seasons, substrates, and symbiotes, and when I am out walking I gladly greet them.

With time and attention, the forest becomes legible. One October afternoon, driving back from a riverbank where a friend and I had foraged without much luck, apart from a glossy brown *Ganoderma oregonense*, I glanced to my right, saw hemlock, Douglas fir, salal, and moss, understood their significance, and pulled off the road. Moments later, we found ourselves among the ruffled gold of chanterelles, brilliant lobster mushrooms, and a pale ribboning *Sparassis* as big as my friend's head. Our hearts sang with the sudden abundance.

Walking the same paths year after year, I learn the seasons and moods of a forest and the names of the living things within it: purple, pear-scented *Cortinarius traganus*, like amethysts in beds of moss; minuscule pink *Mycena pterigena* growing in the whorl of a lady fern; the odorous garlic pinwheel on its black thread of a stalk. Every *Helvella vespertina* is a gracious sculpture, every *Coprinus nivea* a quiet joke. Knowing what I know, it is easy to believe that God looked upon creation and saw that it was good. I can also believe that when He created the species meant to steward His creation, He saw that it was very good.

So it should have been: attention, love, obedience, responsibility. But now "all is seared with trade," Hopkins writes, "bleared, smeared with toil." For profit, we have industrialized, mechanized, and digitized most of the planet.[3] We fail to see things as God did, with His love and contentment, lose respect for His creation, and despoil forests, grasslands, mountains, oceans, and the night sky. Forgetting to whom it belongs, and how to read what is there, we tear page after page from the book of the world.

⌒ↄ

Before literacy became widespread, nature served as a common text. Wisdom literature from every continent refers to the natural world, because nature, unlike scrolls, stelai, courts, or palaces, was open to observation by all.

---

3. This was and remains a common lament among the poets, who are, after all, trained to pay attention. See Wordsworth's "The World Is Too Much with Us," as well as his complaint in the preface to his *Lyrical Ballads*, both of which seem as applicable today as two centuries ago. William Wordsworth, *Lyrical Ballads, with Pastoral and Other Poems*, vol. 1 (London: Longman, Hurst, Rees, and Orme, 1805), xv–xvi.

The Book of Proverbs instructs us to study the ant for her wisdom and marvels at the ways of eagles, snakes, lions, lizards, locusts, rock badgers, goats, and roosters. We who are sliced thinly by the hands of the clock, shod against concrete and asphalt, and screened in by electronic displays would benefit from such marveling, such watching and studying.

If we returned our attention to nature, we would realize that life can never be unvarying happiness under a cloudless sky. It is instead a sifting of sediments, a cracking open, a melting, a solidifying, a structuring. The marsh wrens and blackbirds that swell with song in spring flee before winter for milder climes. The trees that flame glorious crimson and gold soon exchange their splendor for nakedness. The driest season, or the coldest, the thunderstorm, the hail: each afflicts us for a time and passes on. Often, what is left in their wake is opalescence, iridescence, a shining from shook foil.

When I am not careful, patient, and calm in handling their boxes, my bees provide a sharp and white-hot discipline. They taught me that the biblical promise of a land flowing with milk and honey is not an exemption from stings or labor, but a guarantee of both. The promise is that sweetness and nourishment will come after. To the extent that our honey is purchased in jars and our milk in cartons, we miss the millions of flowers, deft thievery, calving, pasturing, and care that are needed for each. We sleep better for the change, but understand less.[4]

"Attention is the beginning of devotion," Mary Oliver writes.[5] Attention is also the beginning of a rich and real life. When we notice how slowly the rings accrete on both mollusk and tree, and how much time is required for all things to grow, we learn patience with ourselves and our own slow growth. When we are startled by the fragrance blowing from winter daphne, sweet woodruff, or honeysuckle, by a snow of cherry petals, or by the fairy fall of cottonwood, we discover a happiness that is both transient and recurring. To see water sometimes impenetrably silver and sometimes a translucent bottle-brown, revealing the grass carp in their secret courses, is to brush against deep mystery.

The catalyzing dose of nature need not be large. For C. S. Lewis, the lid of a tin that his brother heaped with moss, flowers, and twigs opened his eyes to both nature and beauty, tinting his conception of Paradise ever after.[6] But there must be such a dose or encounter to begin with, if one is to wind up with sound theology, a grounded life, or incandescent art. Artists from Leonardo da Vinci onward have criticized those who imitate other artworks

4. Incidentally, I suspect that, from the Byzantines onward, every portrait of John the Baptist, who lived on locusts and wild honey, is lacking in a certain pink puffiness around the face and hands.

5. Oliver, "Upstream," 56.

6. C. S. Lewis, *Surprised by Joy* (New York: Mariner Books, 2012), 7.

rather than observing and experiencing nature for them-selves.[7] Those painters' brushes replicated fad and style, but did not produce a clear and courageous statement of how one human being saw and ordered the world.

Likewise, many who write today imitate other people's writing, swallowing and spitting out a predigested version of the world. Their work does not draw upon what Hopkins calls "the dearest freshness deep down things." Seeing only what has already been seen, parroting only what has already been said, they create, at best, dilutions of other people's visions, and shadows from their light. An osprey chick is fed scraps of fish by its parent until it can fly and hunt on its own. Then it has to hover on the strength of its wings, watch for the motion of life beneath the surface, and plunge for it into the mirror of the lake, to seize what it saw, if it can. Bald eagles will fight ospreys and each other for their catch, and sometimes steal the fish and make a fine meal of it, but I have no admiration for the

---

7. Echoing or possibly alluding to Dante's "Sì che vostr' arte a Dio quasi è nepote" from *Inferno* XI l.105, Leonardo da Vinci asserted that painting is "the grandchild of nature" and "related to God Himself." Artists should not imitate other artworks, he says, "because, by so doing, they will be called grandsons, and not sons of nature, as far as art is concerned." *Artists on Art: From the Fourteenth to the Twentieth Century*, edited by Robert Goldwater and Marco Treves (New York: Pantheon, 1974), 49–50. Similar remarks can be found in the selections from Rubens, Sebastiano Conca, Chardin, Falconet, Hogarth, and Sir Joshua Reynolds, along with remarks from artists who disagree.

theft. Meanwhile, my heart stops in my mouth when the osprey folds its wings into chevrons and falls.

The reader must also observe, learn, taste, and grow, in order to distinguish between gaudy sham and muddy, mossy, living art. There is always a period of being fed, but only the silver living creature will satisfy someone who is fledged, who knows the leaping updraft and the mirror-breaking dive. The same can be said of Christians, who begin with the "milk of the Word" but are meant to progress to more solid food, so that they may be fortified for a powerful work. A seventy-year diet of nothing but milk gives neither strength nor energy. But there are countless Christians in that condition, who sit open-beaked like gull chicks Sunday after Sunday, expecting others to feed them regurgitated mush. They have not yet taken the first step toward discerning for themselves the difference between that which produces life and that which produces death, much less matured to the point of feeding others. Paul was grieved by these infants in Christ (1 Cor. 3:2; Heb. 5:12–14), who preferred stasis to growth.

Such readers, writers, and Christians are in God's hands, not mine. But how I wish for them to awaken to life, to feel the taut sails of their pinions, the wind over the lake, and the fearful freedom of the infinite sky.

For it is freedom we are called to: the freedom of life and flight. The paradox is that flying is made possible by certain intractable laws, from fluid dynamics to gravity, just as living is possible only because of the strict rules governing cell differentiation and replication. It takes time for the fledgling to master those laws and find its balance in the air. But there will come a day when we have learned flight so thoroughly, for the joy of our wings against the wind, that we trust our wings' implicit knowledge of those laws, forget them utterly, and are free.

Chapter Eleven

THE GOLDEN THREAD

L ATE IN HIS LIFE, BALDWIN TOLD THE *VILLAGE VOICE*, "I am working toward the New Jerusalem....I won't live to see it but I do believe in it."[1] The New Jerusalem, the city he was speaking of, belongs to those who are homesick for a place sensed but never seen. It is the city of Hebrews 11 and Revelation 21–22, the crown of the new creation, God's final draft, where His kingdom and kingship are restored. There, a place is prepared for us, a labor

---

1. Interview with Richard Goldstein, "Go the Way Your Blood Beats," *Village Voice* (June 26, 1984), https://www.villagevoice.com/2018/06/22/james-baldwin-on-being-gay-in-america.

of love is waiting, and each will receive a new and secret name. When the world is made new, we will see that city set upon the earth. It is for that end, and not for any muddled and unbiblical conception of heaven, that I and others strive and have striven.[2]

In my mind, the city and kingdom that are to come most resemble the central reality called Timeheart in Diane Duane's *A Book of Night with Moon*. Death carries off character after character, but now and then it becomes apparent that the lost beloved has simply been reassigned to a greater work. For Timeheart, or the kingdom, call it what you will, is nothing but our world perfected and renewed, shining in every lineament. We glimpse it here and there, breaking through, if we look: the trireme of a blue heron sculling through the air, the man who forgave me thousands of dollars in damages to his car as easily as breathing, the mutual prayer that alters the hearts of those in conflict, and the peace that ensues.[3] Whenever

---

2. This position coincides with the views in N. T. Wright, *Surprised by Hope*, and George MacDonald's sermons.

3. In 1917, in a short autobiography serialized in the Toronto monthly *Everywoman's World*, L. M. Montgomery wrote: "It has always seemed to me, ever since early childhood, that, amid all the commonplaces of life, I was very near to a kingdom of ideal beauty. Between it and me hung only a thin veil. I could never draw it quite aside but sometimes a wind fluttered it and I seemed to catch a glimpse of the enchanting realm beyond." She would later borrow the passage for *Emily of New Moon*. L. M. Montgomery, "The Alpine Path: The Story of My Career," 3rd installment, *Everywoman's World* 8, no. 2 (August 1917): 16, https://www.canadiana.ca/view/oocihm.8_06802_56.

we speak, create, act, and move in obedience to the living Spirit within our spirit, we spin out lines of gossamer, imperceptibly fine and yet stronger than steel, that draw that kingdom closer. The bright shadow upon our outstretched hand, we know not how, multiplies the bread and fish we offer, causes one woman's spilt perfume to saturate millennia with its sweet fragrance, and removes the cloaks of past miseries to reveal the blessings beneath. Joseph, embracing the brothers who sold him, tells them truthfully that there is nothing to forgive, for everything has worked for life and good. Time is no obstacle to this reweaving, death no hindrance. Like a chess player of surpassing skill, who has contemplated a million permutations of the game before moving the first pawn, God's teleological view is such that even the past can ripple, shift, and show itself changed, and a desperate situation in the present reverse itself in four moves and end in victory.

By the end of *The Man Who Was Thursday*, G. K. Chesterton's poet-policeman declares that the secret of the world is that we have only seen the back of things. Might history resemble a red-figure bowl, which shows one image on the inside and, if we lift it up, a second portion of the story on the underside? How the man in the pictorial story must have laughed, Karen Blixen says, when he saw how the six ditches he fell into formed the claws of a finer design. How Joseph must have laughed in the morning, when he saw how the pit he was thrown into saved his entire family and a nation besides. How Sarah laughed, the second time, when the unbelievable became true. Because I have seen these revisions in my own life, I too can laugh and praise God for the dark and hopeless places, the bitterness and bruises, now that I see a little of the larger pattern of which they form a part. Never everything — though we are permitted to ask it of God — but enough.

Certain stories and fairy tales, as well as the quest structure, suggest something of what is being done.[4] Seven swans fly over the tumbrel bearing the silent queen to the pyre, as she continues the blistering nettle-work that she was assigned; in the next moment, her brothers are restored to human form and run to her defense. Perceval fails to inquire into mystery and wanders until he learns to ask what should be asked and to pursue what is worthy of pursuit, and thereby heals a king and finds a grail. Such stories remind us that there are laws higher than human laws, and an authority greater than that of kings. That higher law, whose command is love, must be obeyed even to the transgression of the lower ones, and that King of kings may gainsay any other. They also strengthen us against despair. At any moment the faintest gleam in the dark might flame forth as overwhelming light by which the world is set in order.

---

4. See L'Engle, *The Rock That Is Higher*, 229.

For J. R. R. Tolkien, the distinguishing mark of the fairy story is its final turn toward "a piercing glimpse of joy, and heart's desire, that for a moment passes outside the frame, rends indeed the very web of story," so that something of the joy that lies beyond the world spills through.[5] The highest form of it, he says, is that of the gospel:[6] the story of how God loved the world enough to enter into its sufferings and sorrows and humiliations and die in pain and disgrace on our behalf, so that we might become His children, if we choose, and return His love, and work toward His kingdom. The leap from fairy tale to gospel is not so far if we recall that, in Old English, *spell* first denoted any story or prose narrative,[7] then meant a sermon, long before the word came to mean enchantment. The *gospel*, in Old English, was the "good spell," or good story, told to us by Jesus.

The good story ought to transfix and transform us, as we of more modern speech expect spells and stories to do. But like any other story, it can only do so if we allow and assent to such a change. Our freedom to refuse is identical with the freedom to love God and become what His love can make us. That freedom is what was lost in the beginning, then ransomed at high price. Even now He risks our refusal in every moment. The good story, the gospel,

---

5. J. R. R. Tolkien, *On Fairy-Stories* (London: HarperCollins, 2014), 76.
6. Tolkien, *On Fairy-Stories*, 77–78.
7. Tolkien, *On Fairy-Stories*, 48.

is not only a fairy story but a love story, and it ends in marriage: of Creator and creation, of the kingdom of God and the whole of the universe, of story with reality. It is not stained by the sentimentality of the adulterated love or fairy story, but has the terror and power of the original forms. It tells of love as unbearable and consuming as the blast of a forge; the beloved's answer, as beautiful and terrible as an army with banners; and all the evil and destructiveness that has lived in the world since the earliest rebellion, seeking to turn the story from its intended course.

To live as if this story is true, despite our doubts, in spite of the active and encircling darkness and the falsity and cruelty in the world—to believe that every human being is beloved of the Creator, and formed to do a beautiful work that no one else can do, if only she will let that love transform her utterly and set her hands to the task—is to fly through darkness toward a flame. It is, as Baldwin warns us, a total risk of our lives. But the truth is that we are all staking our lives on one thing or another, whether faith in God or faith in the stock market. Ecclesiastes 3:11 tells us that God has put eternity in man's heart, and means for us to seek it, though we will never in our lifetimes find it within our grasp. But the seeker who goes forth in response to that call, not knowing where he is going, will find himself, after many years of weary walking and strange and marvelous sights and sounds, on the banks of a swift river, whose waters are death, seeing in the distance the country of his inheritance.

That is the task. In the end, it is not something we accomplish by our own effort and intention, but by allowing a greater power and love to operate upon us and through us. By so doing, we come to live as if we were already inhabitants of that kingdom, serving as priests and ministers of God (Rev. 1:6; Isa. 61:6; 1 Pet. 2:9), and through our living we make it true. For writers, once language and technique have fused with the intuition, and once the fire of God becomes the scouring source, there is no longer any meaningful separation between the holy life and the writing life. This may be true of every form of art. It may even be true, as Léon Bloy implies, of every act.

I have not written this book to fence off any portion of literature from any other; to proclaim members of an elect and name and denounce others; to argue what cannot be argued, which includes both aesthetic taste and faith; nor to persuade, which is God's responsibility and not mine. I wish to set aflame those for whom the book is written, who will know who they are, with longing for the one light shining out of history and the arts that is older and brighter than all of creation. I am writing to draw closer the kingdom of God. We are each of us Grail knights questing in doubt, fear, hope, and faith for the impossible and the miraculous, which, if we do not turn back, we may glimpse now and again, though as yet far off. Last of all, and most selfishly, I have written this because I desire new novels to have again that light and wildness, the love that orders and frees and the liveliness that astounds, that they might nourish me once more. The stoppage of that spring concerns me. I would have it freely flow.

When I taught composition, it was not easy to convince most students, accustomed to dashing off assigned essays in single drafts, of the worth of revision. But the experienced writer knows that the first draft is rarely the best, that thoughts can be improved and clarified with time and questioning, and that errors are common and become more prominent when revisited a week or a whole month later. Over multiple drafts, the writer sharpens imagery, reveals and differentiates characters, reinterprets events, and facets and polishes language. A river of thought may deposit enough sediment in its course to change from torrent to winding oxbow, and welcome more fish into its waters as a result. In revision, the writer is collaborating with the writer's past self, demolishing whatever is unsuitable, shoring up whatever is unsteady, and measuring, correcting, and adding new rooms. The final structure is usually stronger for having gone through several drafts.

One runs back and forth across the span of the work like a weaver's shuttle, adding with each pass some nearly invisible and yet indispensable line. The soft and enfolding cloth, cut from the loom, bears no evident relation to the fastidious work of shedding, picking, and battening, much less the slow elaboration of a design here or a pattern there. Within the miniature universe of a novel, I have written and rewritten disorder and suffering into an ordered whole, so saturated with meaning that nothing of what has passed, however terrible, is wasted. The project took a decade, and I staked my life on it. Not until the fourth draft did the novel's form become shapely and distinct. If I, as inconsequential as a spider, could do this small thing, why should I not believe that the One presently revising the world can do the same and more? [8]

I have no answers to the questions I ask, nor proof of anything, or the questions would not be worth asking. I have doubts and fears enough for a long night's vigil. But I have also seen, dancing through the works and lives of those writers who have finished a deep, true work, who have opened a magic casement[9] onto the prospect of our world made new, a single golden thread that here brocades

---

8. See L'Engle, *A Stone for a Pillow*, 224.
9. Perhaps the self-same song that found a path
   Through the sad heart of Ruth, when, sick for home,
   She stood in tears amid the alien corn;
   The same that oft-times hath
   Charm'd magic casements, opening on the foam
   Of perilous seas, in faery lands forlorn.
John Keats, "Ode to a Nightingale," in *The Poetical Works of John Keats*, edited by H. Buxton Forman, vol. 2, 3rd ed. (Philadelphia: J. B. Lippincott, 1891), 271.

the surface and there hides beneath the warp. I believe what they have said about it.

I have that golden thread in hand. Often it seems too faint to feel. Then it gives the faintest glimmer or the slightest pull. I have followed it this far, and it has not led me astray. I will, I hope, continue to the end.

ACKNOWLEDGMENTS

I am indebted to Markus Hoffmann for receiving my anomalous book proposal with aplomb, suggesting improvements, and immediately identifying the right home for this book. Daisy Hutton saw the potential in it and took a leap of faith. I had the extraordinary good fortune to be edited by Beth Adams, and the manuscript benefited greatly from her wise and patient advice. Lori Paximadis' incisive copyedits were a delight to receive. The entire team at Worthy Books has been exceptional in every way.

I would not have thought of writing this book were it not for a couple dozen paying subscribers to the newsletter I started as a lark, including Susan Gossman and Misha Stone.

My thanks and gratitude to Atsuo and Izumi Miyake, Jennifer Pan and Michael Lu, and several others, whose warmth, light, and hospitality brought me back to God. For their prayers and friendship, without which my life would be something else entirely, I thank Elizabeth Chen, Esther Chen, Mary Margaret Stevens, and Donna Dannals and her prayer group, who held me up to God, or possibly held up God—I would not put threats past them—while I was in Kabul. Christina Lai sent me *Praising*. Beatrice Njambi taught me that isolation is an illusion. Many, many more have prayed over me, or extended grace and mercy.

To the God of George MacDonald, Flannery O'Connor, Madeleine L'Engle, and James Baldwin, who set me this task and the other one: I'm still cranky at You. Come back later.

As this book should have made clear, I could not be who I am without all the lightbringers who went before me. The same can be said of my family.

ADDITIONAL PERMISSIONS

ABOUT THE AUTHOR

E. Lily Yu is the author of the novel *On Fragile Waves*, which won the Washington State Book Award, and the story collection *Jewel Box*. She received the Artist Trust LaSalle Storyteller Award in 2017 and the Astounding Award for Best New Writer in 2012. She lives in the Pacific Northwest.